Exile

WITHDRAWN

EXILE: A MEMOIR OF 1939

Bronka Schneider

Edited with Forewords by
Erika Bourguignon and Barbara Hill Rigney

OHIO STATE UNIVERSITY PRESS

COLUMBUS

Copyright © 1998 by The Ohio State University. All rights reserved.

[CIP data to come]

Text and jacket design by Paula Newcomb.
Type set in Minion by Tseng Information Systems, Inc.
Printed by [to come].

The paper used in this publication meets the minimum requirements
of the American National Standard for Information Sciences —
Permanence of Paper for Printed Library Materials. ANSI Z39.48-1992.

9 8 7 6 5 4 3 2 1

CONTENTS

ILLUSTRATIONS

Following page 000

Oil painting of Bronka, age eight, Cracow
Bronka, on a visit to her sister, Belgian sea coast, 1937
Bronka's parents, Lasarus and Anna Eichhorn, Vienna, ca. 1930
Joseph with the dog Sheila, "Yearkerscleugh," Scotland, 1939
Bronka and Joseph, Peoria, May 1948
Bronka with her four-year-old nephew Larry in South Orange,
     NJ, 1948
A Jewish man scrubbing a Vienna street in 1938. Part of Alfred
     Hrdlicka's "monument of admonishment against war and
     fascism," near the Vienna State Opera
Burial of Torah scrolls destroyed during Kristallnacht, November
     10, 1938. Central Cemetery, Vienna, Jewish section

FOREWORD

*... this brief chronicle bears within it the force of those docu-
ments which, when they come to light after long years, or even
millenia, become witnesses to the times (and then it makes no
difference what individual they concern) ...*
— *Danilo Kiš*, Hourglass, A Novel

THIS MEMOIR, written more than two decades after the fact, re-
visits an episode in the history of Austrian-Jewish emigration of
the Nazi period that has received scant attention in this country.
Its author, a woman with no claim to being a writer, tells an affect-
ing, personal tale.

Bronka was my aunt, my father's younger sister. She was born
in Cracow, the ancient capital of Poland, in 1899, into a Jewish
family with deep roots in that city. She died in a nursing home
in New Jersey in 1990. She wrote this text in about 1960, when
she and her husband, Joseph, were living in Peoria, Illinois. It was
never published; the *Ladies' Home Journal,* to whom Bronka sent
it, declined publication on the grounds of length, and perhaps also
on the basis of editorial considerations. And so these pages have
remained in the hands of the family.

The memoir tells the story of how Bronka and her husband
spent a year as servants in a Scottish castle. The year was 1939–40
and they were refugees from Vienna. Austria had been annexed by
the German Reich in March of 1938, and the German authorities
quickly made it clear that there was no room for Jews in their lands.
Indeed, we now know that it was Adolf Eichmann's special mission
in Austria to get the Jews out. Goering, in an often-cited remark,

is said to have congratulated the Austrians for having managed to get rid of more Jews in four months than the Germans had in five years. And so Bronka and Joseph and the rest of us searched for a country that might offer a refuge.

Finding a way out under continuously more restrictive conditions was a desperate process; few doors were even slightly ajar. Indeed, at the World Refugee Conference held at Evian in 1938, representatives of thirty-two countries met to discuss the plight of the German Jews and then adjourned without a plan. None were willing to make a major commitment, to offer a haven. When the numbers could be counted after the war, Great Britain had admitted thirty thousand Jews from Austria in the period between March 1938 and the outbreak of the war on September 2, 1939. Bronka and Joseph were among these fortunate few.

One might ask why Barbara Rigney and I trouble to think and write about this document, written more than thirty years ago about events that took place more than half a century ago, and written by an unknown woman who described, for the most part, small events acted out on the stage of one remote household. Except for the story of the escape from Austria, there is little drama or suspense here. Yet we believe that the document has intrinsic interest in that it shows the momentuous events of world history from a particular local point of view, as presented by one observant woman. It adds another small detail to the vast picture of what happened to the Jews of Europe. Bronka's story tells of some who were not annihilated, though many of their friends and relatives were. Joseph's elderly mother and his unmmaried sister, Fanny, were unable to get out. They stayed behind in Vienna and did not survive. One of Bronka's sisters, together with her teen-age daughter, was caught in the Warsaw ghetto; they too did not survive. Bronka's mother, my grandmother, spent the war years in Brussels. Although she did manage to survive, and was able to join her surviving children in the United States after the war, at the time her fate was uncertain. Part of the burden of those in safety was their concern for their loved ones and, for most of them, their inability to act on their behalf.

The Holocaust has been documented extensively. The mass deportations and mass killings have received most of the attention, as of course they must. But the story is larger and more complex. The migrations of those who escaped are part of the story too, not only because they are part of the human struggles but also because they affected the rest of the world in significant ways. The record tells mostly of the famous, those whose lives and works made a significant impact. In the summer of 1996, the ninetieth birthday of the film director Billy Wilder was celebrated in Vienna as well as in the United States, and the memory of Sigmund Freud, the founder of psychoanalysis who escaped to England, presided over the 1st World Congress of Psychotherapy held in Vienna at that time. Another conference, entitled "Hitler's Gift to Britain," also convened in the summer of 1996. But most surviving Viennese Jews were neither Wilder nor Freud. Indeed, most surviving German Jews were or are anonymous — ordinary people, or *kleine Leute,* as Wolfgang Benz calls them in his 1994 book.

In contrast to Benz and other authors to whose work we will refer, we focus on a single couple and on one year in their life of migration. While allowing Bronka to speak for herself, we attempt to provide as much context as possible to enable this one story to shed light on a larger field. In this year in the life of this refugee couple, we hear little, in fact, of what is going on in the wider world. The narrative takes place during the months just before the war and during the "phony war" (the winter of 1939–40), when Poland was invaded but little was happening on the Western Front. It involves a relatively isolated spot in Scotland with a limited but varied cast of characters: the English lady and her husband, a British civil servant retired from his years in India; the Scottish gardner and his wife; other refugees who are servants in other households; a family of evacuees from the slums of Glasgow. And there are great obstacles, ubiquitous differences: in language, in landscape and physical setting, in food and food preparation, in transformations of position and identity. Everything is different, and Bronka is able to consider it, for the most part, with a humorous backward glance.

Now is the time to consider and reconsider these events, while some of us who remember them are still alive. As Arthur Miller wrote in 1996, speaking of his play *The Crucible:* "Fear doesn't travel well; just as it can warp judgment, its absence can diminish memory's truth. What terrifies one generation is likely to bring only a puzzled smile to the next." And he goes on to tell how, in 1964, when the cast of his play *Incident in Vichy* was shown a film of Hitler giving a speech, "they giggled at his overacting" (1996: 159).

Our aim is to reflect both on Bronka's text and on that now remote period. What happened before the Schneiders went to Britain? What was their Vienna like? Who were they, and what kind of lives did they lead? How accurate are Bronka's descriptions; are they confirmed by the accounts of other witnesses? How do ordinary people live in extraordinary times? How do people construct their narratives and construct themselves in and through their accounts? Does it help us to understand a particular segment of a life if we know what came before? What came later? How is it that the ordinary aspects of women's lives can provide essential tools for survival? What of cultural differences—in manners, in outlook, in expectations, not to mention in food—that Bronka prepared in 1939? How do these affect her chances for a successful negotiation of the struggle? Here Bronka shows her observational skills, her humor, and her flexibility.

What have we learned in the past half century that perhaps helps us to see what the participants in these events could not see? There are plenty of questions—we attempt to cope with these and others in the hope of both preserving a human document and of making it available and interesting to others.

Bronka entitled her manuscript "The Other Side of the Fence" and dedicated it "In memory of Grace." The title makes one think that Bronka might have seen Britain, viewed from Austria, as representing the proverbial "greener grass." Instead, we find a small remark speaking of the life of the domestic servant as "the other side of the fence," a side where this middle-class woman did not wish to be but that gave her a new perspective on society. As for

Grace, we are not sure who she was, but the context suggests that she may have been Mrs. Tandie, the kindly wife of the gardner. Bronka was not a writer. We have preserved her words and some of her occasionally awkward English. She gave her husband coauthorship, even priority, but the writing is hers, and she uses the first person singular throughout. He did, I am sure, help her remember particular episodes and encourage her and assist in the development of her text. We don't know how the manuscript came to be written. There is no evidence that she had kept a diary or other record to help her memory. Yet the text follows a clear chronological order. Much of the writing is lively; scenes are set and the narrative is carried on through reconstructed dialogue. The manuscript was composed at a time when Bronka was not employed and seems to have been rather isolated and bored with her life in Peoria. Perhaps it was intended as a project to distract her and to record stories about that Scottish period, so atypical of their lives before and after, stories she had been telling friends and relatives for years. From the perspective of Peoria and her situation there, she is remarkably positive about what must have been a stressful time. Perhaps for Bronka, writing served to put some order into these memories, to make sense of the experience, to create a coherent narrative. Rather than evidence of a positive integration into a new life, it seems to me that this account was Bronka's rather heroic attempt to overcome the past—what the Germans call, on a collective basis, *Vergangenheitsüberwältigung*.

Barbara and I have divided our tasks as editors and commentators in somewhat overlapping fashion. As a family member and survivor of the next generation, I rely on bits of personal knowledge for some comments. Where relevant, I also refer to some items of a vast, ever growing literature in order to provide background and to enlarge the scope of the discussion. We are necessarily selective with regard to the sources we use, since we wish to keep this project within bounds. It is not our aim to present an extended monograph; rather we want to give primacy to Bronka's own account. As an anthropologist, I reflect on some examples of cultural differences and their negotiations. My friend Barbara looks at these materials from her perspective as a literary scholar and specialist in women's writings. By combining and contrasting our different perspectives, drawn from different scholarly backgrounds and different life experiences, we hope to enhance the reader's experience and enjoyment of these pages.

Erika Bourguignon—

References

Benz, Wolfgang, ed. 1994. *Das Exil der kleinen Leute: Alltagserfahrungen deutscher Juden in der Emigration.* Frankfurt a.M.: Fischer Taschenbuch Verlag.

Miller, Arthur. 1996. "Why I Wrote 'The Crucible': An Artist's Answer to Politics." *The New Yorker,* Special Politics Issue, October 21 and 28, 158–64.

ꟻOREWORD

Power is the ability to take one's place in whatever discourse is
essential to action and the right to have one's part matter.
— Carolyn Heilbrun, Writing a Woman's Life

WE HAVE TITLED the following document a "memoir" because
many years intervene between the events recalled and the actual
writing and because it does not constitute a "life" story but a frag-
ment of the writer's experience. That fragment is personal history
recollected, re-collected, reflected upon, and set apart from the
global chaos of its contemporary context, the events surround-
ing the Holocaust (events that Erika Bourguignon elaborates upon
in her introduction and in her commentary following the manu-
script). Like a great deal of twentieth-century literature, Bronka's
memoir is an escape narrative. Documented are the threats, the
fear, the flight to at least a relative safety. But all this happens in
the first few pages, and what is subsequently left unsaid is much
more significant than what is said. The reader, like the editors of
this manuscript, will have many more questions than answers.

Bronka's silences are heavy with significance as she attempts
to construct a personal and historical reality through a shattered
present in which her language and her culture are radically altered
or lost almost totally. One of these remarkable silences is that
Bronka never overtly identifies herself or her husband as Jews, nor
does she ever refer to religious belief, whether her own or that of
any other person in her narrative. Yet her language, her descrip-
tions of daily life, her very existence, are intrinsically based on
her Jewish identity. Contemporary scholars of the Holocaust, in-

cluding Shoshana Felman and Dori Laub in *Testimony: Crises of Witnessing in Literature, Psychoanalysis, and History,* have theorized that survivors of this period, whose accounts are only now being systematically recorded even as the witnesses themselves age and die, are "the bearers of the silence" (viii), refugees from a history that is "at once unspeakable and inarticulate—a history that can no longer be accounted for and formulated on its own terms" (xviii). Bronka rarely cites events of that history once she leaves Vienna. Although she mentions reading newspapers and comments that she and her husband listen to radio broadcasts, she rarely refers to their content. In an attempt to replace Bronka within the historical context she seems to deliberately ignore, we as editors have superimposed on her text, at the beginings of chapters, headlines from the *London Times* for the approximate dates of the events she recounts. How ironic that while Bronka cooks and visits a dentist, while she concerns herself with the neighbors' visits and the Scottish weather, Hitler invades Poland, refugees pour across borders all over the world, and members of her own family die along with unnamed millions.

We can see these silences as maintained in deference to the readers Bronka imagined for her manuscript, but also as protective attempts to evade a devastating consciousness. Felman and Laub speculate that "cultural frames . . . have failed, essentially both to contain and to account for the scale of what has happened in contemporary history" (xv), and that the entirety of the Holocaust "still functions as a cultural secret, a secret which, essentially, we are still keeping from ourselves, through various forms of communal and personal denial" (xix). According to Felman and Laub, all Holocaust testimonies share the nature of being "composed of bits and pieces of a memory that has been overwhelmed by occurrences that have not settled into understanding or remembrance, acts that cannot be constructed as knowledge nor assimilated into full cognition, events in excess of our frames of reference" (5). A similar explanation might be posed for the recently published cookbook edited by Cara De Silva, *In Memory's Kitchen: A Legacy from the Women of Terezin,* which is a collection of recipes gathered by survivors from the victims of this concentration camp north of Prague. Bronka's cooking, which she recounts in great detail and with obvious pleasure, is, like theirs, an act of survival, not only because cooking is part of the job that permits the exit from Austria but also because cooking provides a basic connection to normalcy, domesticity, and therefore to life. It is a claim to sanity in a world surely gone insane.

Erika mentions in her introduction that Bronka was not a writer, and true, her English is not polished and does not flow easily, although there is a kind of poetry in her style. Her language is typical of many European immigrants of that time, the people with whom I grew up in neighborhoods in New York City. There is often a phrase, an inversion of conventional syntax, that strikes me with nostalgia. "No poetry after Auschwitz," as Adorno has stated, and this is partly true of this memoir, which while situated in the picturesque setting of Scotland, contains no poetic descriptions of landscapes, almost no color, no consciousness of beauty beyond the recognition of a few flowers in the neighbor's garden.

Yet poetry lies not only in the extraordinary syntax of a line here or there but also in the fictionalized elements of the narrative. The opening lines, evocative of DuMaurier's *Rebecca,* the setting of an almost Gothic castle in Scotland, and the narrator's stance as naive visitor are all the heart of fiction. We have evidence that the names of people and even of some of the places in Scotland are fictionalized. The "Harringtons" were actually a family named Hamilton, and the town southeast of Glascow is also Hamilton rather than Harrington; the castle was named Gilkencleugh rather than Yearkerscleugh, as we discovered from Bronka's own notation on the back of a photograph (one included in this book).

As Erika states above, Bronka was a talented observer of a too-real world, but her characters share with fictional ones many elements of the fantastic. The Tandies might have emerged from the pages of a Dickens novel, so cozy and quaint is their existence, so nourishing their gifts of food, and so warm their home and hearth. Bronka's employers, too, are fictionalized but never idealized versions of the British gentry with their financial roots in the

Colonial project and their only real cultural association with India (or even with Scotland, for that matter) being concerns about climate or menus available for dinner. These characters and others in Bronka's text are literary stereotypes, all of which would be more comfortable in a novel than in a memoir. Carolyn Heilbrun quotes Roland Barthes's definition of biography: "a novel that dare not speak its name" (28). Thoughts also of Virginia Woolf's *Orlando* are inevitable: "We have done our best to piece out a meagre summary from the charred fragments that remain; but often it has been necessary to speculate, to surmise, and even to make use of the imagination" (119).

Quotation marks frequently indicate dialogues in Bronka's text as they would in fiction, dialogues surely imagined ten years later, for there is no evidence that she kept a diary or attempted to record events at the times they occurred. Bronka's imagination rather than her memory must have inspired these passages, a possibility that enlightens present-day controversies about the role memory plays in narrative creation, about the permeable boundaries of truth and fiction, about the nature of autobiographical writing itself. Bronka's text (as well as Adorno's frightening statement quoted earlier) indicates that, in the aftermath of the events of the 1930s and 1940s, we need to redefine poetry and its relationship to history, not in conventional terms but in terms of reconfigurations of both past and present.

Also crucial for understanding the significance of this manuscript is the basic question of why Bronka felt so compelled to write her experience. Surely it was not for the fame and fortune that might follow publication in the *Ladies' Home Journal,* the popular magazine to which Bronka submitted her manuscript and by which it was rejected. We might conclude, although there is little evidence of this in her text, that Bronka wrote because she felt herself a part of history, and that to record that history, no matter how selectively or with what fictionalized elements, was a kind of trust. Why else, twenty years after the events she narrates, would she consult her husband on details, strive to re-create a place and period with such concentration, remember times and names of trains, record the existence if not the actual names of inconsequential places and people, and, finally, arrange her text so carefully chronologically, month by month? Perhaps Bronka saw her project not as a choice but as a duty, not only to family but to history, maybe even to her self, for through claiming her part in history, writing *her* story, she reclaimed her identity or perhaps even created a new one to correspond with the new life she found in the United States. Although she shared credit for authorship with her husband, as Erika describes above, Bronka herself is the I-narrator, the I-witness, and like the messenger in the Book of Job, she only has escaped alone to tell us.

In spite of this ever-present "I" and this controlling intelligence, this is not a standard confessional autobiography: we have little intimate knowledge of Bronka herself and none at all of her husband, Joseph. We must read between lines to intuit that Bronka is in every sense a survivor; she is not a victim and never sees herself as such. That sense of a strong self permeates her text, dictates her irritabilities (which at times amount to intolerance), and provides humor in what must have been a humorless world. Bronka fusses over English dietary habits, like Mrs. Harrington's insistence on daily doses of rhubarb for her husband's health, and wryly describes her own comical attempts to boil, bake, or stew it to anyone else's liking. She disdains the hygiene of native Scots, one family of whom, to her disgust, uses a bathtub for storing coal. Bronka has little affection for children in general, particularly those in close proximity, and she never had a child of her own. It is Joseph, dressed in his butler's jacket and tie, who plays tennis with the Harrington's granddaughter and seems to love children, as Erika says was true of him in life when he was a favorite uncle.

Thus Bronka is no saint in her own story, and for this I like her quite well enough, although my initial impetus was to conceive her as a heroine. On first reading, for example, I was impressed by the fact that she would not leave Austria without her husband, even though, as she tells us, it would have been easier for a single woman to find employment than for a married couple. I looked for a love story, or at least a hint of such. But Erika, with what may be familial circumspection, disabused me of the possibility of writing my own fictions. "Well . . . ," she said, and the ellipsis indicated more than I wanted to know. Equally revelatory was a comment made by one of Joseph's surviving relatives about the nature of the Schneider marriage: Bronka's sometimes imperious nature was summed up by Joseph's reference to her as "the Duchess of Cracow," an epithet, one imagines, given with humor but also with affection, even with pride.

So Bronka keeps her story her own and eludes every attempt of mine to change her. Whatever creative urges plagued Bronka to write, romantic sensibility was not one of them. As Lawrence Langer warns in *Holocaust Testimonies,* "Auschwitz permanently destroyed the potency of the sedative we call illusion" (4). Nor, try as I might, can I construe Bronka as a protofeminist, despite her female bonding with Mrs. Tandie, unless the very act of writing her own text, claiming her own voice, makes her that. In his essay on autobiography and postmodern theory Clark Blaise states that "every life is a complete cultural history of its time. Every life is a Great Life" (208) — but, I must qualify, only if that life is written.

Bronka's literary ambitions ended with this document. According to Erika, she attempted suicide after the death of her husband but lived into her nineties in a nursing home in New Jersey. The manuscript might never have appeared in print were it not for the coincidence that Erika and I both attended an exhibition entitled "Witness and Legacy: Contemporary Art about the Holocaust" at the Columbus Museum of Art in 1995. Erika commented that she, too, had had a passport marked with a large red "J" like the one exhibited. And then she began to speak, as she never had before in our long acquaintance as colleagues and close friends, about her youthful experiences and her emigration to the United States. She mentioned a manuscript written by her aunt, which I begged to be allowed to read. This book, then, is the result of that fortunate accident and of our fortunate collaboration. Except for this manuscript, Bronka's life is not easily distinguishable from those of millions of other survivors of this terrible period whose stories remain untold and for whom there never was a new Jerusalem.

BARBARA HILL RIGNEY—

References

Blaise, Clark. "Your Nearest Exit May Be Behind You: Autobiography and the Post-Modernist Movement." In *The Seductions of Biography,* ed. Mary Rhiel and David Suchoff, pp. 185–201. New York: Routledge, 1996.

DeSilva, Cara. *In Memory's Kitchen: A Legacy From the Women of Terezin.* Translated by Bianca Steiner Brown. Northvale, N.J.: Jason Aronson, 1996.

Felman, Shoshana, and Dori Laub. *Testimony: Crises of Witnessing in Literature, Psychoanalysis, and History.* New York: Routledge, 1992.

Heilbrun, Carolyn. *Writing a Woman's Life.* New York: Norton, 1988.

Langer, Lawrence L. *Holocaust Testimonies: The Ruins of Memory.* New Haven: Yale University Press, 1991.

Meyers, Odette. *Doors to Madame Marie.* Seattle: University of Washington Press, 1997.

Rosenberg, Blanca. *To Tell At Last: Survival under False Identity, 1941–1945.* Chicago: University of Illinois Press, 1993.

Suleiman, Susan Rubin. *Budapest Diary: In Search of the Motherbook.* Lincoln: University of Nebraska Press, 1997.

Woolf, Virginia. *Orlando.* New York: Harcourt, Brace, Jovanovich, 1928.

*A*CKNOWLEDGMENTS

WE WISH TO thank Bronka's surviving relatives, especially Lawrence Lorre, her nephew and custodian of the manuscript, who has given permission for its publication; Hans Hirsch of Harrow, England, for his own reminiscences and comments as well as information about sources and bibliographic materials; and Joseph's cousin Ludwig Rudel, who provided material and commented on the manuscript. Mr. Francis A. Rankin, archivist of the South Lanarkshire Council of Scotland, also provided valuable information.

We also thank Doris Byer for her gracious hospitality in Vienna and her invaluable help in finding relevant background materials. Mary Maclay Copenhaver was instrumental in getting our contacts in Scotland, in connection with her research into her own Scottish ancestry. Her comments and questions about the manuscript greatly helped us to think through some of the issues involved. There are others who read the manuscript and assisted us with their valuable questions and comments and we are grateful to all of them: Helen Fehervary, Joanne Ziegler, and Robert Beasley.

We are particularly grateful to Julia Katherine Rigney for her initial editorial assistance, her transcription of the rough manuscript, and her research, including the contemporary newspaper headlines that appear at the beginning of each chapter. J. Kimble

Rigney provided valuable assistance with the preparation of the electronic manuscript. Our editor at OSU Press, Charlotte Dihoff, has been unfailing in her support.

The original manuscript has been deposited with YIVO, the Jewish Scientific Institute in New York.

THE OTHER SIDE OF THE FENCE

BY

JOSEPH AND BRONKA SCHNEIDER

In memory of Grace.

(Bronka's original title page)

Joseph and Bronka Schneider
2024 N. Gale Avenue
Peoria, Illinois

Approximately about
4,000 words

The other side of the fence
by
Joseph and Bronka Schneider

Not long ago we received the sad news that Yearkerscleugh is no more. It burned to the ground, and though four fire brigades were trying to save it, they didn't succeed.

Many a year has gone by since we came to this place, but by reading the letter which told us about the end, all our memories came back to life, and here is the story.

(Bronka's original cover letter)

Germany Mobilises Industry

"... It can be said without presumption that no other country in the world surpasses Germany in the systematic adjustment of economic life to military requirements," Herr Rudolf Brinkmann.
— *London Times*, January 1, 1939

Dr. Goebbels on Hitler's Critics

" 'The Year 1938 was the most successful of the Nazi regime — an unforgettable year in German history' — declared Dr. Goebbels."
— *London Times*, January 5, 1939

Refugees Seek Factories
Permits Delayed

— *London Times*, January 8, 1939

Reichstag Speech To-Day
German Attacks on British Press

"Berlin is preparing to celebrate Hitler's assumption of power and the first meeting of the Great German Reichstag. ..."
— *London Times*, January 29, 1939

~ 1 ~

I SHALL NEVER FORGET the moment we received our permit enabling us to go to Britain into domestic service. Not that we were anxious to be domestic servants; we never held that kind of job before, but it was the only possibility of getting out of Austria.

It was February 1939, almost a year since the German Nazis

invaded our country, and aided by a considerable number of Austrian Nazis, continued the murder of innocent people. There was terrible fear: concentration camps, people picked up off the street never to see their families again. Women were taken from their homes to wash the sidewalks; no means of persecution were low enough to break our spirits. I myself was hit by a woman, spat on by a man for no reason whatever, and no one could do anything about it. We were without rights, without any kind of protection; no court or judge would have taken our case.

It was time to get out of the country, but where to go. The United States had a quota system, and the country where my husband was born had such a low immigration quota that it would have taken years of waiting. Other countries allowed some refugees to enter; a number of people tried, in order to save their lives, to go to neighboring countries without a permit or visa. A few of them managed to stay, but many were turned back right into the arms of the Gestapo.

Then one day I heard from a friend that there existed a possibility to go to England if one found a job as a cook or maid or as any kind of domestic servant and if the people who were providing the job would be willing to apply for the permit.

It was a long drawn out procedure, and not everybody was willing to go to all that trouble, especially when they didn't know what kind of people we were and whether we would be able to do the job. Once they applied for the permit they had the responsibility to provide the work whether they liked us or not. There was a risk involved, and one could hardly blame anybody if he didn't feel up to it.

There were also much greater difficulties in finding a job for a couple; a single girl or woman could get a job much easier. But we were determined to try. We sent in ads to the English papers and took a course in a special school for domestic servants. My husband learned how to become a butler, and I tried to improve my cooking.

There was no response from the English papers that would amount to anything, but we did not and could not give up. It was our only possibility to escape the Nazis. We felt there was no other way out. We talked and asked friends and anybody we knew who also was trying to find some means of escape, what to do and where to go. One day a friend, who explored different English agencies, gave us an address of a person in Scotland who was in contact with an agency for domestic help in Edinburgh. Even though she knew we had never been domestic servants and did not know whether we would be able to work in an English household, she was willing to help.

And so we wrote to that person, not knowing whether it was a man or a woman. We knew so very little English then that by the name alone we could not tell whether it was a man's or a woman's name. We addressed the letter: Dear Sir, and with the help of a dictionary and some friends, we asked her help in finding a job. The Sir was not a Sir but a woman; she wrote a very friendly but not very encouraging letter that it would be extremely difficult to find a job for a couple and advised me to try to find a job for myself. Once I had a place, it might be easier to get my husband out too.

She enclosed the name and address of the agency in Edinburgh and told us to get in touch with her. I could not decide to ask for a job for myself, as the men were in much greater danger. We decided to ask her to help us both and assured her how hard we would try to do our best in these strange circumstances if we could only have the chance. We waited and prayed and hoped for an answer, but none came for a long, long time.

And then came the 10th of November, a day that none of us should ever forget, the day the Nazi party officially dedicated itself to murder and Synagogue burning, to dragging defenseless men out of their homes, taking all their possessions away. Most of our friends were picked up, put on trucks like cattle, and driven off to concentration camps. Any minute now we expected the S.A. man to come to our apartment and get my husband. He waited for them, put even his old coat on, but nobody came. It was about five o' clock in the afternoon when the atrocities that were going on since early morning were called off; the men who were on the truck already were sent home, and it seemed just like a miracle was happening.

For the time being my husband was safe, but who could tell

for how long. We had lost, like all the others, the means to make a living; everything seemed to close in on us, no place to go and no hope to stay and stay alive. In our despair we wrote again to Mrs. Gilbert who gave us the address of the employment agency. We let her know what was really going on and asked her again to explain to the agency our urgent need for help.

About two weeks later came a postcard which looked like insignificant printed matter that my husband almost disposed of. But looking at it again, he decided to show it to me. And there it was, the unbelievable, wonderful news that a job had been found for the two of us. That was all the card said, no name of our employer, no sign when we could expect the permit; but just the same it was wonderful to know that there was hope. After the first excitement subsided, we got very anxious to know more about our job and wrote again to the agency asking for more details. No response.

My brother and his family managed to go to Switzerland, where they were awaiting their visa for the U.S.A. We asked him to write to the agency, hoping he could find out what we could not. And it really worked. We received an answer from Edinburgh advising us that the job as butler and cook had been secured for us with a Mr. and Mrs. Harrington. But Mr. and Mrs. Harrington, though they had applied for our permit, were now on vacation, and the matter would be somehow delayed. Now was the time to be patient and wait for some news from our future employers. We waited in constant fear, and as it seemed that we waited long enough and heard nothing from them, we decided to write to Mr. and Mrs. Harrington. Again, with the help of one of our friends, we wrote a letter asking for an answer as to whether there was any hope of getting the permit in the near future.

Within ten days came a very short and matter of fact letter saying only that all the necessary steps have been taken to obtain a permit. That letter in our state of mind gave us quite a scare; it was so cold and without any personal approach. But that feeling only stayed with us a short while, and then all we saw was freedom.

That freedom was not quite at hand yet. We still had to wait. It seemed that all we did was wait from one day to another, and these days seemed more like years. Though we realized we were better off than most of the others, having at least the promise of a job and a permit, our nerves were still very much on edge. Every time the mailman came, we would run to the door hoping that it might be the day for the permit to arrive.

In order to make some preparations for our future jobs, we took English lessons. I had some advantage over my husband as I had English lessons before, while my husband didn't know a word of English. As we could not afford to pay for lessons, a very good friend of ours who spoke English well was willing to make him familiar with at least some sentences which might be of help to him to get along at first. It was very difficult for him to study because he was in such a tense state of mind, though he tried very hard. We even managed to get a few laughs when we compared our English with some friends who knew as much or as little as we did. There were sentences like: The lady is good, The lion is strong, The picture hangs on the wall, sentences which would not be of great help in our new surroundings, but we tried not to worry too much about that. Somehow we would manage if we only had the permit and could get out.

Aid for "No-Man's Land" Jews

"The Jews, who have been in no-man's land on the German-Polish frontier since the end of November, are to be allowed to return to Germany to settle up their businesses. . . . The Jews are to be allowed to return and after settling their affairs will be permitted to take certain movable articles out of the country with them. . . ."
— *London Times,* January 29, 1939

Scientists and Refugees
Move by Learned Bodies, Posts for 900 Scholars

"The Royal Society, the British Academy, and the Royal Institution are all joining in the launching of an appeal by the Society for the Protection of Science and Learning for funds to assist the large numbers of refugee scholars. . . ."
— *London Times,* February 5, 1939

German Mobilisation Rumours Are False

"Rumours of sudden German mobilisation are so frequent that soon nobody will believe them. . . ."
— *London Times,* February 19, 1939

~ 2 ~

AND THEN THE day came. It was six months since we tried to find a job in England. Six months of hoping, fear and waiting. It was one afternoon when our mailman brought a registered letter, and we knew right away that was it. Later on one of our neighbors remarked to us: "You must have received wonderful news; the mailman told us that when he gave you the mail today, your face was radiant." Indeed it was wonderful news for us.

We carried the permit around with us showing it to our friends, and we noticed how happy they were for us as they did not quite believe that this dream of ours would ever come true but never tried to discourage our hopes.

There was still a great deal of endurance in front of us before we could leave; now that we had the permit we had to have the passport. In order to get a passport, we had to prove that we paid our taxes and did not owe anything to anybody. That in itself would not have been difficult to prove, but the procedure in which it had to be done was meant to persecute and humiliate us. We were not treated like citizens who only a few months ago were just ordinary people with the same rights, but as outcasts who ought to be glad if they were only allowed to walk the streets. We had to stand in line for hours in order to obtain the necessary papers; every day were new decrees. When we thought that we had satisfied every and each of their moods, here it was again: new photos showing a particular side of one's face, and a great big J. on the passport signifying that one was a Jew.

All these sadistic wishes of theirs took days and days of lining up. Once I came as far as the door of the Internal Revenue Office after hours of waiting, the doorman shut the door in my face saying: "It's lunch time, come back tomorrow morning." And the next day I had to stand in line all over again. The waiting and the lining up we took in stride; we even had enough sense of humor to smile about these mean ways of our enemies. But what was connected with it was the way they treated us once we were inside the office: the questions, the remarks. One never knew what would happen next, and that part was hard to take. But we took that ordeal too, and when we look back and know what had happened later, how our people who could not leave the country were massacred, we realized that these persecutions we suffered were little and were meant to satisfy the ambitions of small and insignificant people who thought it was their chance now to show us who the master really was.

The day finally came when we had everything ready; our passports and visas were in order. We sold our furniture for almost nothing, and some of our belongings we sent away, but these were later confiscated by the Nazis. All we could take with us were our personal belongings and ten Austrian shillings each. Now came the sad part. As much as we were longing for the day to leave and were busy preparing for our departure, now we were all ready to go, but the thought of having to do so and leave our friends and relatives behind came to us with such a clarity that all of a sudden the joy of being able to save ourselves from the murderous hands of the Nazis was gone. We were going to try to help our loved ones escape; once we were in England, though, we knew there was little hope. But even if they had to stay, we could not imagine that the Nazis would do to them what they did. Nobody could have thought of the horrible cruelties committed on the old folks and children which were to come, those which left the inhuman mark forever on humanity.

Nearly 250,000 Jews Leave Germany
Majority Go to US
—*London Times,* February 26, 1939

Germany's Campaign for the Nation's Health
"Health and how to safeguard it has become one of the main topics of conversation in the German capital where every household has this year experienced unprecedented attacks of flu.... Even Herr Hitler suffered from the illness...."
—*London Times,* March 12, 1939

WE LEFT ON the 12th of March, 1939. The train on which we were leaving could have been called a heartbreak train. There were children whose departure was made possible by some committees in different countries, but whose parents had no place to go. These parents, though glad for their children, were crying their hearts out knowing that they would probably never see their faces again. We also had to go through an ordeal of saying good bye to our family and friends, who would not let us leave without seeing us off.

Our journey was uncomfortable as long as we were in the Nazi occupied country. Before we came to the border, we had to go through a very strict censorship, like criminals we had to strip and be searched for treasures. As if we would have dared to take anything along that was not officially permitted. We lived through that degradation too.

Antwerp, Belgium was our first stop, and what a joy it was to be out of that Nazi hell. We stayed there for two weeks with my mother, who went to Belgium to seek refuge from the Nazis. From there we sent a letter to Mrs. Harrington informing her that we were on our way to England. What a pleasant surprise it was to receive the most friendly answer in which she explained that she wrote her first letter in such an impersonal way because she was afraid that we might get in difficulties corresponding with a foreign country. She urged us to come as soon as possible, as there was a great deal of talk about a possible war, and if we waited too long we might not be able to cross the border. We noticed from the letter that they had a car, and as we never had one, my husband thought that he had better have some driving lessons while we were still in Belgium as that might be one of his duties. But fortunately that was not required of him.

We said good bye to my mother with great sadness, but at least for the time being, although she was alone, she was better off in Belgium. We went to Ostende, and from there we took a boat to Dover. On the evening of March 27th, we arrived in London where we were met by my husband's cousin, and with whom we stayed for three days. They too were refugees from Germany, but already had a nice apartment, and seemed to be settled. One thing that we first noticed and that surprised us in their apartment was an open fireplace. At first we thought it was for decoration purposes. It looked so warm and cozy. But our cousin explained that it was more than that; it was the thing that actually heated their place. We had never seen a fireplace before, unless in some pictures. Our apartments and houses were heated by stoves and some had central heating. Our cousin told us they were as surprised as we, but they got used to it and liked it. Well, that was our first experience in England.

The ten Austrian shillings that each was allowed to take out of the country did not go very far. The Bloomsbury House in London was a committee created for the purpose of helping refugees from Nazi oppression. Next day we registered with them, along with hundreds of other people, and spent a whole day there reporting to different offices. Everybody was very kind, and before the day was over we were treated like human beings again. We received one pound English money and the railway ticket to our destination in

Scotland. When the man gave us the money we thanked him; he also said "thank you," which seemed strange to us, but which was, as we were told by my cousin, the British way of being polite.

We notified Mrs. Harrington of our arrival in London, and asked for directions and information about how to get to their place. She replied that she would meet us at a station called Lymington in Scotland, and that she would know us as she saw our pictures at the employment agency when she hired us.

The short time we spent in London seemed wonderful to us; we could again walk the streets without being afraid. But the few days went by fast, and we had to leave for our destination. The thought of it made us feel uneasy. We had not the slightest idea what the place we were going to would be like, whether we would live in the country or in a town. We had never been in contact with English people before and did not know their ways and habits. The only consolation was that they did not know anything about us either, and that at least would put us on equal footing. And so we left and hoped for the best.

On the train, a man started, or let's say tried to start, a conversation with us. That poor guy had quite a time to do so, and so did we. He wrote a sentence or two on a piece of paper in the hope that we might be able to understand better, and in a few mutual attempts by using our hands too, we got across to each other. We made him understand where we were going, why, and what kind of a job we had accepted. He seemed very sorry for us, and said it would be a very hard job, especially because we had never had experience working in other people's homes. He was very kind and gave us his address in case we got into some kind of trouble and needed help. But we never really did.

Imminence of War

WE WERE QUITE nervous by the time we arrived in Lymington. There were very few people at the station, but one of them was Mrs. Harrington. She came towards us and asked us if we were Mr. and Mrs. Schneider. She talked very quietly and must have felt as uncomfortable as we did. She smiled and asked about our luggage, and when she saw it she said to take only the small suitcases along, and she would have our trunk brought in later. To my surprise I understood what she was saying.

And so we started our journey to Yearkerscleugh. Mrs. Harrington drove the car; we sat in the back, and nobody was saying anything. Mrs. Harrington was a nice looking middle-aged woman, dressed in a tailored brown coat and matching hat.

We drove and drove, it seemed for hours, and all was country, few farms and a few homes. As we have always lived in the city and only spent our vacations in the mountains, this country with the strange-looking bare hills and miles and miles of nothing made a very depressing impression on us and did not contribute favorably to our mood.

Finally we came to a lovely little village with pretty homes, a few stores, and a few people on the street, and we hoped that here was where Mrs. Harrington's house was located. The name of the village was Arlington. But our hopes were shattered when

Mrs. Harrington did not stop, but only continued to drive on and on. We could not ask how much farther we will have to go, we wouldn't know how, and Mrs. Harrington didn't speak. She must have noticed that we were quite bewildered and kept silent.

As we were driving a while longer, we noticed a big sign on the road that said, "Harrington." It was the same name as that of our employers, and my husband and I looked at each other having the same thought, that the Harringtons must be important people because they had the sign showing the way to their place. We later found out that Harrington was a town and the sign was related to it.

Suddenly Mrs. Harrington turned into a big open gate that led into beautiful and spacious grounds, and we found ourselves in front of a very historical-looking castle. In front of the huge carved door stood a smiling elderly lady in a black suit. As Mrs. Harrington did not introduce her, I thought she was one of us and almost asked her to help us with the suitcases. But I didn't, and it was a good thing too because she was one of Mrs. Harrington's sisters. We entered a hall, and for a moment we just stood there looking. It was very large and paneled with wood from the ceiling to the floor. From the hall led a stairway to the upper floor, and for the time being that was all we could take in. A strange feeling descended on us: no one we knew had ever lived in a place like that. Back home were castles too, but these were only visited by sightseers.

Mrs. Harrington showed us into the kitchen, which almost took my breath away. It was a very large country kitchen; a big black coal stove occupied a whole wall, and a huge hunk of coal was burning in the middle of it. Everything was sparkling clean, the range polished to high gloss, and my first thought was: "How in the world am I going to keep this place as it is now and cook on that enormous thing?"

But Mrs. Harrington came to my rescue and directed my attention to a good-sized oil stove that looked somehow like our gas stove at home, and that made me feel a little bit better. There was no gas in the country, and even the electricity had to be worked by hand. Mrs. Harrington told us where we could find the tea and suggested we have cake, which was already on the table. And then she handed us a letter that had come the same morning from a friend in Vienna. She left us alone for a while, realizing that we might want to read the letter and get over the first shock.

While we read the letter, I started to cry. I couldn't help it; the letter made me feel so homesick, and now I realized that we had lost everything, that we were in a strange country among strange people, and we even had to share the roof with them whom we had never met before. Why did all that happen to us? My husband listened to me and, though he was as upset as I, he said: "How many people would give anything in this world to be in our place and have a roof over their heads?" These few words brought me to my senses, and when Mrs. Harrington came in and said she would take us to our room, I was all right again.

It was a big room on top of the stairs with an adjoining bathroom. The fireplace was lit, but it was not very warm in there. There were two beds, a chest of drawers with a mirror, a little table and two easy chairs in front of the fireplace, and a very small wardrobe for our clothes. I could not figure out how we would place our clothes in that wardrobe and had in mind to ask Mrs. Harrington for a larger one but decided to do it at a later date. Our trunk arrived while we were in the kitchen, so we didn't see who brought it up.

We unpacked a few things and went downstairs again to see whether we should prepare supper. Everything was so quiet, we didn't even know how many people were in the house. Mrs. Harrington came and told us that she had prepared supper already but she wanted us to come to the dining room where she would show us how to lay [set] the table. She said there would be three of them, she and her two sisters. The dining room was large and had seven windows all on the same wall, a big fireplace, and on the opposite wall from the windows were pictures, a gallery of Mrs. Harrington's ancestors. A long table stood in the center, a few pieces of furniture, and on the long buffet we saw very beautiful pieces of silver.

We wondered where Mr. Harrington was, but we couldn't ask her. The supper consisted of soup, a vegetable dish, and baked apples. From the pantry there was a ledge to the dining room through which I put the dishes, and my husband took it from here. It was his first experience as a butler. He had to place everything in front of Mrs. Harrington. She again put the food on the plates, gave it to my husband, and he put it in front of the person it was meant for. After supper, we washed the dishes in a little pantry, and when Mrs. Harrington told us we could go up to our room if we wanted to, we were very glad as we were very tired from the trip and all the excitement. Before we went up, she told us to come down around 8 o'clock and she would show me how to prepare breakfast and show my husband how to light the fire in the fireplace. And so ended our first day in Yearkerscleugh.

We tried to go to sleep but felt cold and homesick and miserable. Though we realized how lucky we were to have escaped our persecutors, we could not be happy thinking of our friends and relatives back home. We were determined to do our best here, but it would be difficult to concentrate on cooking and cleaning while our people were afraid of everybody who knocked at their door. And we knew how terrible it was to have to be afraid.

Easter in Germany
From Our Berlin Correspondent

". . . In Berlin, Germans can buy slightly over 6½ ounces of butter per head per week on their butter cards, which leaves little that can be used to bake the famous Easter cake."
— *London Times,* April 9, 1939

Herr Hitler's Birthday
Berlin Plans 5-Mile "River of Light"

— *London Times,* April 16, 1939

∼ 5 ∼

MRS. HARRINGTON's older sister had breakfast in bed, which I took up to her accompanied by Mrs. Harrington. She greeted me in a very friendly way, and I wished I knew what they were thinking of me. When the others had breakfast, Mrs. Harrington asked me if I would like porridge and bacon, but we only wanted tea and toast. At that time I didn't think we would ever be able to eat that kind of breakfast, but I was mistaken. The house work and the country air made us so very hungry that we were grateful to have a substantial breakfast, and after a few more weeks I even liked the kippers and haddock.

We cleared the table, and I washed the dishes while my husband was to clean the dining room and parlor. This room was so large that it had two fireplaces, one on each end of the room, but only one was in use. My husband never held a vacuum cleaner in his hands before. Back home the men never helped with the housework. Most people had maids, and we also had a daily help. But he was handy and soon got used to that kind of work. When I, who had less difficulty with the language, asked him how he managed to understand what Mrs. Harrington was saying to him, he replied, "Oh, it's all right. If I do the wrong thing she smiles and shows me how to do it right, and if I still don't do it the way she explained, than she smiles even more and leaves the room." Mrs. Harrington smiled most of the time and never got mad, and if she did, we never knew it. Somehow the work was done; it just took a little longer in the beginning.

Off the kitchen was another little room that was called the larder. All the names, like pantry, scullery, and larder, were new to us. In the larder were kept some dishes and some food. We had our own milk and butter that came from a near by farm while the milk and butter that Mrs. Harrington was using came in sealed bottles by train from some town. We also had our own bread, cake and jam. I thought it was a strange arrangement but it was probably the way things were done in this part of the world.

Next I had to go to Mrs. Harrington's bedroom and help her make the bed. It was the first time she called me by my first name. We only called our best friends and our servants by their first names. And as I wasn't Mrs. Harrington's best friend, I was her servant. And it was then that I felt a little pang in the vicinity of my stomach and, though I knew we were hired as domestic servants, I couldn't help feeling a slight resentment at being on the other side of the fence. We also noticed that my husband was not Mr. Schneider anymore, but just Schneider.

I had to get over that feeling. It was a job like any other. There was nothing degrading about it; we just had not done anything like that before, and that was all there was to it. And, as the time went on, we accepted being called by our first names and even found it amusing.

Mrs. Harrington and I went to the bedroom through the hall and up the wide beautiful stairway. The bedroom was large, had seven windows, but unlike the dining room the windows were on all three walls and offered a lovely view out to the grounds. How we admired that view; in winter it was like something in a fairy tale.

The bed was very roomy, seemed quite comfortable and really took two people to make it. Especially difficult for me was to handle the heavy blankets. At home, we had down quilts which were slipped into a fitting linen cover and were very light weight. Struggling with all the blankets, pushing them under the mattress, was quite a chore. After the bed was made, my husband came in to clean the room. There was no open fire in the bedroom; the central heating was supposed to warm it, but it didn't quite succeed.

Next to the bedroom was a large bath room that my husband had to clean too; but first, I had to clean the bath tub. We went then to the room where I took the breakfast the same morning and made the bed. The one bed, where the other sister slept, we didn't have to make; she liked to do it herself. Making the beds for the ladies, there came a question to my mind: "Where was Mr. Harrington?"

I recalled that when we received the news in Vienna that a job had been secured for us, we understood that we would be working for a Mr. and Mrs. Harrington. Had we had sufficient knowledge of the English language, we might have asked a lot of questions as we were anxious to know: how many rooms were here, who occupied the house besides the three ladies, who lit the fire in the basement, who brought the potatoes into the house so early in the morning, and how did all the other groceries get here, as the only stores we saw were in the town. As Mrs. Harrington did not supply any information yet, all we could do was wait and see.

After these two beds were made, Mrs. Harrington told us to make ours and come back to the kitchen where we would make the menu for the day. She, in the meantime, went to her room to get dressed. While we were planning the meals, I soon realized that this was a very economical household, or it seemed that way to me. When we made a dessert at home we thought nothing of using up to ten eggs, but Mrs. Harrington would only go as far as using two eggs.

One thing I realized was that I had to learn to cook all over again. Not that it was so complicated here, only quite different. As a matter of fact, the food was quite monotonous. On Sundays, we either had a joint of beef or a leg of lamb, which usually lasted into the middle of next week. First we ate it warm, then we ate it cold, and later it was made into a shepherd's pie or some other variety. The rest of the week, we had sometimes fish or other kind[s] of meat.

The menus usually consisted of meat, vegetables, and pudding for lunch. Soup, which came in packages in powdered form, eggs or a vegetable dish and baked apples or pudding was for supper. Around four was tea time, which we enjoyed as it was just like home only that we had coffee instead.

When the menu was settled, Mrs. Harrington asked me to come with her to the back of the scullery where there was another room and two adjoining rooms. The larger room was furnished with a table, a few chairs, and again two easy chairs by the fireplace. There also was a radio or wireless. That, Mrs. Harrington told me, would be our sitting room where we could relax and listen to the wireless. I was very pleasantly surprised and thanked her, and when I told my husband about it, he was delighted and could hardly wait to go and listen to the news.

In the beginning I used to go to our room to rest before tea time, but later on Mrs. Harrington found a recipe for home-made scones, which we liked so very much, but I had to make them fresh for tea, and then I couldn't have my little nap. On days like that, I often envied Sheila, who could sleep and lay around whenever she pleased. Sheila was Mrs. Harrington's pet, a grey terrier who ignored everybody except Mrs. Harrington. When she was sometimes left with us, she would not come into the kitchen to have her meal. Oh, no, we had to feed her in the parlor room. Though we were very fond of animals, and in our loneliness we would have appreciated the companionship of a dog, there somehow never developed a great love between Sheila and us.

And so the days went by. After dinner when the dishes were washed, we went into the sitting room and listened eagerly to the radio. It seemed to us, even though it was such a short time since we left home, like many months had gone by, and we were cut off from the whole world, while so many things were going on.

We worried terribly about our people we had to leave behind; we promised to do something for them and wanted, after we had been here a little while longer, to approach Mrs. Harrington and ask her if she could in any way help us.

There was one thing that bothered my husband very much. He just had to know who the mysterious person was who attended to the central heating every morning. Whoever it was came very early in the morning and left before we came downstairs. One morning my husband came down before I was even dressed and said that today he is going to find out. It just didn't seem right to live in a house and not know what was going on. By the time I came down, he was quite excited and told me that he had met a man in the cellar. He couldn't get his name, but when my husband greeted him with a "good morning," the man said something like "nice day;" that seemed strange to me, but maybe it *was* a nice day.

The mystery was solved so far, but we still didn't know who the man was and where he lived. We decided I should ask Mrs. Harrington, and when I did, she said: "That is Mr. Tandie; he is our gardener and he and Mrs. Tandie live in one of those little houses outside the grounds."

The same day, after lunch, Mrs. Harrington suggested we should take a walk and get to know our surroundings. We thought it was a good idea, and after we rested a little while, we put on our coats and left; it was the first time since we arrived that we went out of doors. It was a nice day, just as Mr. Tandie said, but there was no sunshine. We walked around the grounds and looked at the castle from all directions. One part of the castle was built in the sixteenth century, but another part didn't seem so old, and we were told later that it was added in more recent years. It looked very beautiful, surrounded by old trees and very spacious grounds, which were kept up with great care. It was almost unbelievable that only one man could do the job.

Outside the gate was a lonely road; across the gate down the road were two small neat looking cottages, and we assumed that Mr. and Mrs. Tandie occupied one of these. Not a soul was on the road; not even a car passed by, just the two of us. Miles and miles of pastures with grazing sheep and those sad looking hills around them. Though it was April already, all the hedges and trees were still yellow; I remarked to my husband that I couldn't imagine that spring would ever come to this part of the country, and that all this that is such [a] depressing color now will ever turn green. But it did, only a little later than we were accustomed to.

Next morning while I was busy in the scullery, Mr. Tandie came in. I hadn't met him yet, but assumed it was he. He was a man in his sixties, rather thin with reddish hair. I said "good morning," but again he said something that sounded like "grand day." He brought potatoes that must have just come out of the ground because they were full of dirt. Then he spoke again, and so I tried to concentrate on what he was saying, but I just couldn't understand one single word.

This same morning, while Mrs. Harrington and I were making her bed, I felt more courageous to ask a question. I asked her how she happened to hire us for the job. She said she was looking for domestic help and she got in touch with the agency in Edinburgh, and the woman in charge suggested she consider some of the people who applied for jobs and came from Germany or Austria. She gave her about a hundred snapshots to look at, and Mrs. Harrington decided she liked ours best.

She felt quite talkative that morning and mentioned that she was expecting Mr. Harrington in about two weeks' time and that she would go to London to meet him. I was glad to know that there was a Mr. Harrington, although I still didn't know where he would be coming from and what his business was. But in time we would know that too.

By now quite a few of our questions were answered: we knew that there was a Mr. and Mrs. Tandie and that he was the gardener, also that he was the one who brought potatoes each morning. We were also told that the groceries were delivered to the house by the butcher who came twice a week, the baker who came every other day, and the fruit man who came once a week. Before they came, Mrs. Harrington made a list of what to get, and I went out and, partly by showing the list and partly by talking, got the things together.

When I noticed that Mrs. Harrington felt like talking, I took the opportunity to ask her if we could have a larger wardrobe as we had to leave most of our clothes in the trunk, and as it was all the possessions we had, we were afraid they would get ruined. Mrs. Harrington said she realized it and would do something about it before she left for London.

Later on when she came into the kitchen, she said that now that Mr. Harrington was coming home soon she would like me to learn how to prepare the dishes he preferred. One of them was rhubarb. There was rhubarb in the garden, and she would have Mr. Tandie bring it in, and we would start to practice. Every day now I cooked rhubarb. I tried it in a double boiler, in the oven, on top of the stove, and to me it always tasted the same, plain rhubarb.

We got into the habit of taking walks before tea time, and that afternoon we explored the road to the other direction. It was a pleasant day, the sun was out, rabbits ran round us from all sides. We had never seen that kind of rabbit before; now and then when we went hiking in the Vienna woods we saw a hare. There seemed to be lots of them here and at least they were some company.

We walked for a while and came to a good sized house that looked to be a farm. In the garden, with her back to us, stood a woman. She was bending over beds of vegetables. She was a big woman, wore a hat, and the way she stood there offered a funny picture. All one could see was her large hat and her large back. She must have heard us approach because she halfway turned around and, just like Mr. Tandie, said, "grand day."

Above the house were also hills and pastures. A young man and a dog stood there, and both of them were trying to get the sheep into one place. We watched them; it was quite a fascinating procedure, and after they succeeded we turned around and went home again.

We were ready for our afternoon tea and then started to prepare supper. Mrs. Harrington's sisters were still with us; we didn't know whether they would make their permanent home with Mrs. Harrington. We only knew they were not married, because Mrs. Harrington kept referring to them as Miss Graig. We would have liked to have known their first names so we could tell who we were talking about, but again we didn't like to ask. So we gave them first names which we, of course, kept to ourselves, but that way we at least knew which was which. We knew two women in Vienna who reminded us of the two Miss Graig. The older one was short and grey-haired just like the one here; her name was Fanny and the name of the thin tall one was Gisela. And from that day on their names became the ones of the two Miss Graig.

Our days followed now a certain pattern: making a fire, cooking breakfast, cleaning, making beds, and so on. Every morning before I came downstairs, my husband had the fire going in that big black range. The sight of that thing still frightened me. When I tried to cook on top of it, the food either burned or didn't cook, and so I took refuge in the more familiar oil stove. We were still very lonesome, our only connection to the world being the small wireless. We had nobody to talk to, only Mr. Tandie sometimes in the morning, whom we could not understand and who by now had quite a variety of days, like, "Nice day, grand day, dull day, fine day." We were quite amazed at all the descriptions of the days.

And then one afternoon, we met Mrs. Tandie. We were coming out of the gate and onto the road when we saw a woman stepping out of the little cottage and coming towards us. Though it was quite chilly and we had our coats on, she only wore a housedress and an apron. She walked fast, and when she reached us she said she was Mrs. Tandie and shook hands with us. She was a woman in her late fifties, medium height, and round all over. She talked loud and smiled all over her round bright face; she radiated so much warmth and friendliness, and though we didn't know what she was saying, we had a wonderful feeling that she wanted to welcome us. And as she kept on talking and laughing and pointing towards her house, I knew that she wanted us to visit with them as soon as we could. We thanked her and made her understand that we would be happy to come.

After she left us and we walked towards home, we didn't feel so alone anymore. We were sure that we had found someone who we would be able to talk to and confide in and ask all the questions we wanted. It was a good feeling. Only one thing puzzled me. And when I said to my husband, "I wonder why we have such a hard time knowing what Mr. and Mrs. Tandie are saying while it is much easier to understand Mrs. Harrington or Miss Graig?" He was not of great help when he replied, "As far as I am concerned, I have plenty of trouble to understand either of them."

We laughed about his remark, but I still thought there must be some reason for it. And then it occurred to me that Mrs. Harrington must be speaking the proper English like that I learned in Vienna, while the Tandies spoke probably with a Scotch accent. We didn't know enough yet of the English language to distinguish the difference, though we could notice a rolling of the R's when the Tandies spoke; so that must have been it.

A few days later, Mrs. Harrington told us that Mrs. Tandie would like to have us for tea the next Sunday and meet her daughter who works as a nurse in a hospital in Glasgow and who is spending the weekend with her parents. We were looking forward very much to the visit, and when Sunday arrived we dressed nicely and went over to the Tandies' house. It was a real "grand day," the sun was out, and there was a table set in the back garden where Mrs. Tandie and a young girl met us. Shirley was a pretty girl with reddish hair like her father's. She looked and acted like him too, rather quiet, not so vivacious as her mother. We sat there, had tea and delicious homemade scones, and little cakes, and we all tried to make conversation. We listened carefully to what Mrs. Tandie was saying so we might understand, and we really did, and got brave enough to ask some questions. Shirley, in her quiet way, spoke more precisely, and when she said something and she noticed that we didn't get it, she repeated it again.

In the course of that afternoon, we learned quite a few things, things that we could not have asked Mrs. Harrington. By the time we left, we knew that Mr. Harrington was coming back from India where he lived and had worked as a civil servant for twenty-five years. Mrs. Harrington lived there with him for about fifteen years where she met and married him. He was her second husband, and she had two children by her first marriage, a son and a daughter both married and living in India too. There was also a granddaughter, the daughter of Mrs. Harrington's daughter, who was in a boarding school near London and whose name was Patricia. Mr. Harrington was retiring from service and that was why they acquired the "Big house" as Mrs. Tandie called it. It belonged many years ago to the Harrington ancestors and so Mr. and Mrs. Harrington thought it was a nice comfortable place to retire.

We had a very enjoyable time, and when the time came to leave, Mrs. Tandie spoke again very fast, and when Shirley noticed in the expression on our faces that we didn't know what her mother was saying, she explained that she wanted us to understand that we were always welcome to spend our Sunday afternoon in her house and have tea with them. She also told us that if we wanted to go for a longer walk we could go in the direction of the farm to a little village called Crafton-Ann. The other direction led to Arlington, the pretty village we saw coming with Mrs. Harrington to Yearkerscleugh.

Next morning when I was busy in the kitchen, my husband seemed deep in thoughts, and when I asked him why he interrupted his daily routine; he said that Mrs. Harrington told him to go out to the little place in the little garden and give Mr.Tandie a hand. "Why should I give Mr. Tandie my hand now?" he asked. "After all, I met Mr. Tandie some time ago, and we shook hands then."

I didn't know what to say; we didn't want to ask Mrs. Harrington, but it seemed to me that I had heard that expression somewhere before. I took our dictionary and remarked to my husband, "I wonder if that is not one of these phrases that means something entirely different." And here it was: "To give or lend a hand means to help somebody do something." And so I advised my husband to go and find Mr. Tandie and help him with whatever he was doing. After an hour or so, my husband came back and told me he had to give Mr. Tandie a hand with pumping the electricity for the house. Well, we learned something new again.

On our next Sunday afternoon, it was again a pleasant day, so we walked towards the little village of Crafton-Ann. We walked for almost an hour without meeting anybody. The village seemed very old and was so small, one could hardly call it a village. There were only very few houses and a little store, which we saw was open. The woman who owned the store lived there, and as it was the only entrance to her house, she had to keep it open even on a Sunday. She was very friendly; she already knew who we were, so it seemed that word got around about us. We were probably the first people to come across the British Channel to that hidden place.

We looked around in the store and bought some picture cards. One could find anything and everything in that little place. But how the woman could keep track of all these small items, that was beyond me.

On our way back we stopped at Mrs. Tandie's. She had already the table set, this time in the house; it was chilly outside, and in the house the fire was burning and it was warm and cozy. We noticed that the fireplace had two things attached to it that looked like plates on handles and were movable. When we inquired what these were for, Mrs. Tandie put a pot on each of them to demonstrate to us that she did some of her cooking there. When she saw our astonished faces, she took us to the back of the house where, in a pantry, she also had an oil stove only a little smaller than that in Mrs. Harrington's house.

In the other cottage lived a young couple, Mr. and Mrs. Engles. Mr. Engles' business kept him away from home all day, and Mrs. Engles came over to join us and get acquainted. The conversation got a little easier now, and Mrs. Tandie told us that the people who owned the farm and whose name was Galloway also hired a young woman from Germany who was supposed to arrive in the near future. We were very pleased to hear that now we would be able to talk to somebody in our own language.

It was already late in April, and Mr. Harrington was due to arrive from India. Mrs. Harrington was getting ready to leave. Two days before her departure there came a van and some men were unloading some furniture and taking it upstairs to an empty room across from our bedroom. When all the pieces were placed,

Mrs. Harrington told me that this would be our dressing room, and she hoped that we would have enough space for our belongings. I had only asked for a wardrobe, and besides the wardrobe here was a chest of drawers and even a small desk. We appreciated it very much, and I said so to Mrs. Harrington.

Mrs. Harrington was to stay in London about a fortnight and was then to return with Mr. Harrington. We were left with Miss Gisela; Miss Fanny was leaving for her home. We were looking forward to these two weeks. Miss Gisela was on a very strict diet and ate very little. We thought we would have a good rest, but it wasn't so.

Miss Gisela wanted to be a nice sister-in-law and made me try out different kinds of dishes, even some recipes from Vienna, until she took a fancy to one of them. It was a pudding made of cream of wheat; they called it semolina, and it was served with a hot chocolate sauce. She liked it so well that she wanted me to make it on the first day when Mr. Harrington arrived.

She also insisted that we clean the rooms even more thoroughly than we did when Mrs. Harrington was at home. She talked to us more than usual and told us that during the summer vacation little Patricia would come to spend a few weeks with her grandparents. Also Patricia's parents were expected for the summer from India. Miss Gisela took us around the house, showing us rooms where they would be staying.

An entirely new flight of rooms and bath rooms opened to us and we asked how many rooms in all. "Twenty-two rooms and twelve bath rooms," Miss Gisela said. When she saw how surprised and scared we looked, she said, laughing, "Well, not all of them are ever in use." Miss Gisela was quite a nice sort of person; we would have liked to talk to her more, but the language was still a handicap and to keep up a conversation was strenuous for both sides. We were glad to hear that there would be visitors coming for the summer, and, even though it would mean more work for us, we were so eager to have more people around that we would put up with it.

As Miss Gisela was satisfied with the new pudding and also with the way the house looked, we asked if we could have an afternoon off. We had never been to Arlington yet and would like to see the village. We prepared everything for the afternoon tea in case we should be late in getting back. She didn't mind, and we went off. Arlington was about three miles from Yearkerscleugh, and it took us over an hour to get there. The village looked to us, after the lonely place we came from, almost like a town. There were nice little stores, a hotel, and a post office where they also sold candies and stationary. We went into the post office; everyone seemed to know who we were, and all were very helpful and kind.

The town also had a railway station where one could take a train to Edinburgh or Glasgow. One couple we knew from home also had a job like ours in Aberdeen, Scotland. We asked Mrs. Harrington how we could get together, and she said that once a month, if we wanted to, we could arrange to meet them either in Edinburgh or in Glasgow, which were about the same distance from their place as from ours.

We looked around Arlington for a while longer, mailed some letters, and started on our way home. When we were almost half way from Arlington, there came a car; a man was driving it. As soon as he saw us, he stopped and asked where we were going, and when we told him he said he was headed the same way and could take us home. He was very friendly, and, as we were quite tired, we got in and drove with him. After driving for a while we noticed that the car seemed to swagger a little, one way and then the other like it would lose its balance. The man didn't stop talking and it dawned on us that he was drunk. We got panicky and tried to make him understand that we would rather walk, but nothing doing. He didn't pay any attention to what we were saying; he was so friendly and happy and kept on driving. He said he knew where Yearkerscleugh was and was determined to bring us to the door. When he finally did, Miss Gisela opened the door, and when he saw her he got out of the car and in the most charming way greeted her and wanted to come in. But Miss Gisela soon noticed what was wrong with him, and in the same charming way, adding some diplomatic talk, got rid of him.

That was quite an exciting experience in that part of the world where there never seemed anything to get excited about. We even decided to tell the story to Mrs. Tandie on our next visit to her house.

We got used, by now, to tell[ing] her everything. She would always listen and always had something nice to say. I don't know how we could have managed without her. On our Sundays off, we would go to her house like we would go home after a week of work and loneliness. She was like a mother and a friend. She was always cheerful, always busy, but never too busy to give us a smile, whistling and talking while serving her delicious cakes and pastries.

We confided in her that we were quite nervous about Mr. Harrington's arrival, but she said there was nothing to be nervous about. She was sure everything would be all right; he was just an ordinary human being. We left her feeling much better; as usual, Mrs. Tandie's overflowing kindness and understanding gave us a lift.

Mr. and Mrs. Harrington arrived on a rather gloomy day. We were told by Miss Gisela that she expected them in a day or two. But she must have gotten news of the day of their arrival as she told me what to prepare for dinner and to make sure that the semolina pudding should be the highlight of the meal. I promised to do my best.

She was as excited as we were, though we had more reason to be excited. We didn't know what his reaction towards us would be. We got used by now to Mrs. Harrington and the other two ladies of English descent, but an Englishman might be more complicated and especially one who just returned from India. India to us was not the same as to the English people; we thought of it as a different world one never really went to but only read about.

Mr. Harrington turned out to be, just as Mrs. Tandie said, a nice human being with a sense of humor. He was a good looking man in his early sixties who seemed to look forward to his retirement, though I couldn't help wondering what he was going to do with all his free time. He brought all kinds of crazy things from India, some strange looking costumes, and some fierce looking leopard skins with big heads and open mouths showing all the teeth. Mrs. Harrington didn't seem to like these animals, but she was very happy to have Mr. Harrington home.

We set the table in the dining room for three, Mrs. Harrington on one end of the table, Mr. Harrington on the other, and Miss Gisela in the middle. The table was so huge we were wondering how the Harringtons were going to communicate with each other without raising their voices. I was also afraid that by the time my husband served the food from one end of the table to the other, Mr. Harrington would have to eat his meal lukewarm. It didn't make sense to us why they had to sit so far apart. But what didn't make sense to us must have made sense to them.

Miss Gisela left after a few days to join Miss Fanny, and the Harringtons were alone. They were still sitting at each end of the table, until one day my husband came with the news that, though he set the table as usual, Mr. Harrington moved his plate and set himself close to Mrs. Harrington. Well, he was a sensible man.

Mr. Harrington occupied his own bedroom. I had to make his bed, and as the weather was still cold and damp, I had to put each night hot water bottles into the beds. It seemed that Mr. Harrington had some difficulties adjusting himself to the damp climate, probably because he came from India where it must have been very hot. The difference in the climate made him very ill in the beginning; he even ran a temperature. The only thing that seemed to help him was whiskey, which he kept on his night table. The thing that did not help him were cigarettes, but he smoked a great deal. He smoked in bed, in the bathroom, and even caused some damage to a bathroom chair because he left the stub on the chair and forgot it there. When Mrs. Harrington noticed the hole in the chair, she was very unhappy about it, but still she smiled and said, "Oh, these cigarettes." I almost told her one day, "It's not the cigarettes, it's Mr. Harrington," but that wouldn't do.

We understood that the English people who were in the civil service in India had quite a number of servants at their disposal. It was quite probable that one of them was assigned to look after Mr. Harrington's cigarettes and what he did with the stubs. Here there were only the two of us, and we had plenty of work as it was. We could only hope, along with Mrs. Harrington, that Mr. Harrington would not set the castle on fire, and he didn't. As time went by, he got more careful.

Mrs. Harrington had a problem what to do with the leopard skins. She didn't grow fonder of them, and I saw her place one of them in a back room which she very seldom entered. One day I went to our dressing room to fetch something, and when I opened the door, there was one of those beasts laying on the floor and staring at me with its wide open mouth. It scared me so that I ran out of the room. I had no idea that Mrs. Harrington had put one of those things up there. She was coming down, and when she met me on the stairs and saw my face, she asked if anything was wrong. When I told her, she seemed embarrassed; she thought I would like to have one, and she meant it to be a surprise. Well, a surprise it really was, I thought to myself. Mrs. Harrington said if I didn't want it, she would remove it right away, but by that time I had recovered from the shock and was sorry that Mrs. Harrington felt bad about it. I told her it was foolish of me to get scared of a dead animal, and I would like it to stay there as the floor was bare and needed something. Now that I know it is up there, it won't scare me anymore.

But I was mistaken. Every time I went in there, that beast did something to me until I decided to turn it around so that its head would face the wall and not the door. I only hoped that Mrs. Harrington would not go in there, as I did not want to hurt her feelings.

Now that Mr. Harrington was home, Mrs. Harrington wished to plan the meals more carefully. We still had the usual roast or leg of lamb, but now we added Yorkshire pudding to it. That Yorkshire pudding worried me a great deal. I always assumed that a pudding was something fluffy, made with a lot of eggs, more like a soufflé. When I was given the recipe, I made it exactly the way it was supposed to be made. It came out nice and brown on top but the moment one put a spoon inside it, it was mushy and soft, and I didn't think I baked it long enough. I blamed myself but couldn't figure out what I did wrong. Just the same Mr. and Mrs. Harrington seemed to like it, but we did not. My husband said that I must be wrong somewhere and I should ask Mrs. Tandie the next time I saw her. And when I did so, she said to my surprise, "Nothing is wrong with your Yorkshire pudding; that's the way it's supposed to be."

When the butcher came the same week, Mrs. Harrington told me to get some stewing beef so we could have English stew. She put potatoes, onions, carrots and the meat in a pot and poured too much water over it, and, though it tasted pretty good, it looked more like a soup than a stew. I suggested Mrs. Harrington should let me try to make the Viennese stew that we called gulyasch. Mrs. Harrington agreed readily. Since my semolina pudding was such a great success, she liked to taste more of my recipes.

I fried the onions golden brown, put the meat in, put salt and paprika with it, and let it stew without adding any water at first. After the meat juice was used up, I added a little water at a time and let it cook until it was tender. They loved it, and whenever we were to have stew, we would have gulyasch instead. Mrs. Harrington taught me then how to make a meat pudding, a dish which was also made from beef-stewing meat. She made a pastry using suet, rolled it out, and lined a deep bowl with it. The raw meat mixed with onions, salt, and pepper was put into the pastry-lined bowl, covered with the remaining pastry, and sealed with a specially made cover which was made out of a piece of cotton material and had a drawstring to it. Then the bowl was set in a pot with boiling water and steamed for about four hours. The result was very good.

An apple pudding could also be made that way, and that tasted really delicious. Now I introduced our apple strudel, which was a lot of work, but which the Harringtons enjoyed too. And so we got along as good as could be expected.

It was May already. The yellow hedges and trees began to turn green, and the world around us would have looked friendlier if it hadn't been for the news we received from home. There the situation grew worse from day to day. Our friends and relatives never gave up hope that we would be able to help them, and so far we couldn't do a thing for them. We have written to London and committees in Glasgow, but all we heard from them was very discouraging.

We were desperate. We lived here in freedom and in a world that was as far away from Hitler as we were from India. Of course they knew all about him. When we talked to the Tandies, they listened full of sympathy, but they could not help us. And no one who didn't experience the agony of fear could really know what it meant.

The news on the radio was bad too; people couldn't help thinking of the possibility of war, though it really was just a thought. In their hearts, they still hoped there was a way to make peace. We knew better; we knew there was no peace possible with Hitler, unless the Western countries agreed to give in to everything he demanded. There was nothing left for us to do but to write to our people asking them to have patience and keep on trying to do something for them.

**Danzig May Proclaim Its Annexation
Rumoured Nazi Plan**

— *London Times,* May 7, 1939

**No Compromise By Germany
Hope of Weakening in British Policy
Growing Bitterness Towards Poland**

— *London Times,* June 11, 1939

~ 6 ~

AND WE CONTINUED to cook, clean, wash dishes, and all there was to do. Now that Mrs. Harrington wanted to please Mr. Harrington, we had to have rhubarb every single day. Every night my husband would bring in the empty plates into the pantry until one evening someone left the rhubarb untouched on the plate. I asked him if Mrs. Harrington didn't feel well. I took it for granted that it was she who didn't eat it; Mr. Harrington, being so fond of rhubarb, couldn't have left it. But my husband said, "No, it wasn't Mrs. Harrington, it was Mr. Harrington who didn't want it." "What do you mean he didn't want it, he loves it." "Well," my husband said, "when I was about to take his plate away, the rhubarb was still there. And when I hesitated, Mr. Harrington asked me, 'Do you like rhubarb?' and when I answered, 'Not too much,' he said, 'I hate it.'"

I asked him then how Mrs. Harrington felt about it; she must have been upset, after all she tried so hard to please him. But Mrs. Harrington was not in the room at that moment, and what

39

happened when she returned we never knew. We never had rhubarb from that day on.

One morning we were awakened by some noises on the floor where the Harringtons' bedrooms were. It was about five-thirty. My husband got up and looked down and saw Mrs. Harrington in her coat and slippers moving around. There was also a pantry on that floor, and he saw her coming out of there. We wondered if one of them wasn't feeling well; we thought of Mr. Harrington in particular who still seemed to have trouble getting used to the climate. I even meant to go downstairs and ask if I could be of any help, but after all they might not like me to interfere. Should they want us, they probably would say so. We noticed by now that the Harringtons are very controlled; they guarded their privacy and never would show their emotions. To us, it was something we had to get used to; where we came from people were more outspoken. When one didn't feel well, one said so and liked it if other people felt sorry for him.

When the Harringtons came down to breakfast, they looked the same as each morning, and so I thought that there was nothing wrong with either of them. But my curiosity got the better of me, and, when I helped Mrs. Harrington with her bed, I just had to ask if she or Mr. Harrington were sick last night. It would have bothered me all day. She looked very astonished and said, "We were not ill; we were feeling fine; what made you think so?" And when I told her that we heard them moving around at such an unusual hour, she replied, "I was making early tea. We have it every morning about this time, only this morning I forgot to fill the tea jar and had to fetch it from the pantry." "Early tea," I asked, "what is that?" "Early tea is tea one drinks early in the morning, before breakfast," she replied smiling.

She must have thought I was stupid asking questions like that, but how was I to know? And now I also knew what these little oil burners that the Harringtons kept on the table next to their beds were for. To make it quite sure, I asked her again, "I guess these oil burners are for making early tea?" "Yes," Mrs. Harrington replied, laughing heartily. "We probably have some strange habits to you, but in time you will get used to them, and if you feel like having an early cup of tea, have one; it's good for you."

When I reported the incident to my husband, he said to me, "Come to think of it, my grandfather, who lived in Eastern Europe, used to have what they would call here early tea. He used to get up around five o'clock in the morning and have breakfast, but about an hour before breakfast, he had a glass of tea. Not tea with milk as the Harringtons take it, but just plain tea with sugar." In Eastern Europe, people drank their tea in glasses instead of cups; we were reminiscing about our early youth, and I recollected that my grandmother used to drink hot water with milk each morning before breakfast. Well, why didn't I think of it before; I guess it is because it was such a long time ago. "Do you think we have some English blood in us?" I asked my husband, but he laughed and said, "I doubt that very much."

It was quite natural that we would tell Mrs. Tandie everything that happened during the week. It was so easy to talk to her. She was more like we were, not reserved, and liked to talk about everything. It was good to be with her. And when we told her that Sunday about early tea, she laughed and said she thought everyone had early tea.

Both Mr. and Mrs. Tandie were always ready to answer any question we asked. And so I asked how it was that Mr. and Mrs. Harrington were so reserved; we could never be sure if we had done anything wrong, as they never let us know. "Well," Mrs. Tandie said, "most of the English people are reserved." "But you are not that way," I said, "and you are English too." "No, we are not English; we are Scotch," she replied. "But aren't Scotch English too?" "We are all British subjects," she said, "but still we are Scotch, and they are English."

I had to be satisfied with that answer, but on the way home I said to my husband, "Things are getting more complicated, and the things that Mrs. Tandie said do not make sense to me; does it to you? "I believe it does," he said, "but one thing I know for sure, we don't know enough about the history of England or rather Britain, and we will have to get to know more about it." "They know just as little about us," I remarked. "Don't you see," he said, "they don't have to; they didn't have to come to our country, but we had to come to theirs."

The following week was quite uneventful, and, when Sunday arrived, we were again with Mrs. Tandie. She said that today she would ask us some questions. We assured her that we would be happy to answer them as far as we could. She wanted to know what our life in Vienna was [like], what business my husband was in, how we spent our Sundays and vacations. We told her that life in Vienna was very pleasant. My husband owned a store where he sold shoe leather and leather fittings. But business was not very good and I worked too. I had a job as a bookkeeper in an insurance office. Though we were not rich, we could enjoy the theater, concerts and coffee houses, which played an important part in Vienna. In the evenings we met our friends in the coffee houses; in summer one could sit outside, and we sat and talked until late in the evening. In early spring and fall, we spent our Sundays hiking in the Vienna woods, and in summer we shared a little cottage on the Danube where we spent our weekends.

Life was good in Vienna until Hitler came and took everything away. We were not allowed to go swimming in the Danube, and we were not allowed to go hiking anymore. No theater was accessible to us; life just stopped.

Mr. and Mrs. Tandie didn't say anything for a while, until Mrs. Tandie came close to me and said, "Don't take it too hard; we know that the life you have to lead now is not easy for both of you, but at least you are safe here and among friends, and you will not always have to be domestic servants."

One morning shortly after breakfast, my husband came into the kitchen from the dining room carrying a basket on his arm. He told me that Mrs. Harrington asked him to get potatoes, as Mr. Tandie couldn't bring any this morning, so he was going along to the farm to get some. It was a "nice day." I was glad for him that he could take a little time off and take a walk to the farm.

Through the scullery window, I watched him walking through the gate and crossing the road to the side where the Tandies had their little cottage. And, as he was turning towards the farm, I could see Mrs. Tandie coming out of her house in rather a hurry, and, as he saw her, he stopped. I saw her talking to him, pointing towards her house, and he smiling and trying to walk towards the farm. But she still talked and seemed to get very excited about something, when my husband must have decided that he had to be on his way, and the last I could see was that Mrs. Tandie joined him.

About half an hour later, they both came back to the house. My husband had potatoes in the basket; they were clean, not like the ones Mr. Tandie brought every morning. Mrs. Harrington was in the kitchen, looked at the potatoes, at my husband, and then at Mrs. Tandie I thought it strange that Mrs. Tandie came back with him to the house. He put the basket on the table and went to the dining room to continue his cleaning. As soon as my husband left, these two women started to talk. Mrs. Harrington seemed to ask some questions, and Mrs. Tandie answered, but that conversation took place at such a fast tempo that I could not understand one word of what was said. And both of them started laughing, and I just stood there and didn't know what to do.

When they finally realized that I didn't have the slightest notion of what was going on, Mrs. Harrington explained to me that she told my husband to get the potatoes, but she didn't tell him to go to the farm. She took it for granted that he knew that the potatoes came from the Tandies' kitchen garden. And when Mrs. Tandie, who was expecting him, noticed that he was heading for the farm, she tried to stop him but he couldn't understand her. He was determined to go to the farm, and she saw that there was no use; she followed him in order to tell Mrs. Galloway what happened and to ask her to give him potatoes without any questions so that he should not be embarrassed.

I also got a great deal of fun out of that story, but my poor husband was still unsuspecting what mistake he had made, and I had to tell him. And when I did he was very discouraged about how many difficulties he had with the language; but all of a sudden, he started to laugh, and he said, "Now I know why Mrs. Tandie got so worked up. I wondered why every time I started to walk she started to talk faster and faster. I have to thank her that she came along with me; I would have been lost there, Mrs. Galloway not knowing anything about the potatoes."

He asked me if I think he should apologize to Mrs. Harrington for his mistake; he thought it would be uncomfortable for him to face the Harringtons while he served supper; but after we talked about it, we decided he should just leave it at that. It won't be the last mistake and we can't apologize each time. "But you haven't made any yet," he said to me. "Don't worry," I replied, "I will and then it will probably be one that will surpass all of yours." Though we were pretty sure that Mrs. Harrington shared the incident with Mr. Harrington and that both have had fun, it was never mentioned in front of my husband again.

I then told Mrs. Tandie how much I wanted to go to the United States and be reunited with at least some of our nearest relatives who lived out there, but with all the quota restrictions it would probably take years before we could go.

The same Sunday we also heard from the Tandies that Mrs. Peters, who was hired by the owners of the farm, was expected in about a fortnight to arrive from Germany. Mrs. Tandie said that Mrs. Peters had some advantage over us because she did some domestic work in Germany; she held the position of a house keeper to a widower and his son. We wanted to know whether her husband would come with her, but as far as we knew, she was coming alone.

The grounds and trees around Yearkerscleugh became more beautiful each day. They were of deep green, and the lawn looked just like a carpet. The grounds next to one side of the castle were arranged like an open air stage; one could imagine that Shakespearean plays were performed here a long, long time ago.

With weather becoming warmer, Mr. Harrington's health seemed to improve, and he took up a hobby. Every morning after breakfast, he went to the woods to chop wood for the fireplace. The fire had to be kept up every day; the house was pretty chilly in spite of the central heating. Usually Mr. Harrington came back from the woods after my husband cleaned the morning room, and he brought a great deal of dirt in on his shoes.

Again Mrs. Harrington asked my husband to clean it up and said, "Oh, that dirt." Again, I felt very much tempted to tell her that it wasn't the dirt, but Mr. Harrington who was to blame. But I didn't. I don't think it would have helped anyway.

Slowly, the flowers began to bloom, little flowers we had never seen at home. They were of various colors and various kinds. Mr. Tandie explained to us that these flowers lasted one month, and as soon as they were gone, different ones were growing in their place, which again lasted a month, so that all summer long we had different sorts of flowers.

Mr. Tandie kept the grounds in perfect shape, but he could not do it all. One part in the back of the house was overgrown with weeds, and the kitchen garden had to be neglected too. It was too much for one man. The Tandies told us that the people the Harringtons bought the "Big House" from, used to have three gardeners and quite a few servants. They entertained a lot and had garden and hunting parties, but had to give it all up because they had difficulties in finding and keeping the right kind of servants who would stay in this lonesome place so far away from everything.

Mr. Harrington was very fond of cheese and especially blue cheese. He ended his supper every evening with a piece, and, as nobody else was supposed to have any of it, we used to call it "Mr. Harrington's cheese." One evening after supper, my husband told me, "I have learned something new while I served the cheese." "Good for you," I said. "Let me in on it."

"Mr. Harrington asked for some paprika which he wanted on his cheese, and while I handed it to him I made the remark to be careful as it was quite sharp."

My husband used the exact translation from the German word "scharf," which was said in connection with paprika and other spices. Then Mrs. Harrington said it was not sharp, and I insisted that it was very sharp, so he took a knife and touched the blade and said, "That is sharp, but paprika is hot." "I thought that only food that was cooked or the weather could be hot," I said. "And so did I," my husband said.

It was a good explanation, and we both wished the Harringtons would correct us more often, but my husband was right when he said, "They would have to be very busy doing it, and we would never get any work done." Our English needed a lot of improvement, but we could only learn the hard way.

As Mr. Harrington regained his health and the weather was nice, Mrs. Harrington told us they intended to drive to Edinburgh in the next few days and they would be happy to take us along. It would just be for the day, and we would be home again in the evening. We were very happy and excited about the prospect of seeing a city again and especially Edinburgh of which we heard a great deal. We told Mrs. Harrington how much we were looking forward to it and so it was settled.

My husband and I made plans for what we wanted to do in that one day. First of all, we wanted to go see the lady from the agency who got us the job with the Harringtons, because it was the least we could do to thank her in person. Then we intended to go to a good restaurant, to have a fine lunch, sit at a table and have a waiter wait on us. After lunch, I wanted to have my hair done, as I didn't do a good job setting it myself. And of course we planned to look around the city and see the famous castle.

We left pretty early in the morning, had a pleasant ride, and Mrs. Harrington said they would leave us off at Princes Street, that is located in the heart of the city. We were to meet them again at five o'clock. We arrived in Edinburgh around ten-thirty; the city made a great impression on us. Princes Street is a beautiful street. On one side are all sorts of stores, and on the other side is a park, and the castle is on top of the hill that stretches from the park. It is a lovely sight.

We felt so good; the weather was perfect; the women were dressed well; it was like a different world altogether. We started to walk along Princes Street and tried to find the agency. It was not easy, and we had to ask some people for directions. They had a hard time to know which street we meant, but again they were kind and patient and we finally found what we were looking for.

The office into which we stepped was dark and small. There were a few young girls looking for jobs and talking to a middle aged woman in a dark dress talking very quietly. When we told her who we were, she told the girls to wait and took us to an adjoining room. She said she was glad to see us and asked us how we liked our job. We told her we were glad to be here and wanted to thank her for what she has done for us. And then she said almost the same thing that Mrs. Tandie told us before: "You are safe now, and that's all that counts for the moment. You will find jobs that you are more used to and won't have to remain in domestic service."

When we said good-bye, she thanked us for coming to see her and wished us good luck. How friendly she was and how modest. After all, she actually saved our lives, and, without saying much, she knew how we felt and whatever she did, she did it as a matter of course. Before we left we asked if she could recommend a nice place for lunch. She recommended one in the Princes Street, a small but elegant place; the food there was excellent and, though the prices there were high, we didn't care. We knew that it would be quite a while before we came back to this lovely city, and so we wanted to live up a little.

I also had my hair set while my husband took a walk. By the time I got out of the beauty parlor, it was late to visit the castle, and we had to let it go for now; but we were hoping to do it some day. We still had some time to do some window shopping, and then we had to hurry to meet Mr. and Mrs. Harrington. They arrived almost at the same time as we did, and then we started on our way home. We told them how much we enjoyed the day, and Mrs. Harrington suggested that we get in touch with our friends and meet them on our next trip to Glasgow. We could have the whole day off as soon as we heard from them. We came home tired but happy with a prospect to see a big city again. And we were looking forward to meeting our friends.

Next day we wrote to them, and a few days later received their reply saying they could meet us in four weeks in Glasgow. That would be the second week in June. We then settled the time the train would arrive and the place of our meeting and waited for the day.

By the end of May, Mrs. Peters was expected, and Mrs. Tandie was to meet her in a nearby town. Two days after her arrival, the constable who came to see us when we arrived and who took our data and checked our passports, came again and asked me if I would go with him over to the farm to see Mrs. Peters. She didn't seem to understand what he wanted to know, and he was just not able to make her understand. So I was to be the interpreter. The constable was a big man in his forties, and when we first saw him, we were quite afraid of him because whenever we saw a uniform we got scared. But he was a nice and friendly man. He asked me to get into his car and we drove to the farm.

I had not met Mrs. Peters yet and had to explain to her in German who I was and why I was there. She was a young woman, small, very pretty and with a sweet expression. While I was talking to her, I noticed that she didn't hear very well. I had to repeat what I was saying to her. The constable got all the information he needed and took me home. Before I left, I told Mrs. Peters that my husband and I will drop in after supper to visit with her for a little while.

When we came later in the evening, she was wiping the dishes. I could see right away that she was fast in her work and quite experienced in what she was doing and thought that her employers made a very wise choice in hiring her. The farm house, of course, was not to be compared to our castle, but it had plenty of work there too. We couldn't stay too long, but promised Mrs. Peters that we would pick her up next Sunday for a walk and take her along to Mrs. Tandie's house. We were going to ask Mrs. Tandie if that was all right with her, but before we even did, she suggested it herself.

Two months have passed now since we came to Yearkerscleugh; everything went pretty smoothly, only Mrs. Harrington had the habit of giving too many orders at the same time. She told my husband to do one thing, and, before he even started, she wanted him to do something else again. The same applied to me. When she and I made the menu for the day, she all of a sudden would tell me to clean the hall or go upstairs and do something else again. I had to do the cooking under her supervision, which was just a waste of time because by now I was perfectly able to do it the way she wanted it. There was no system, and it created more work and less accomplishment.

It was the beginning of the week one day when I got all my courage together and asked her to make the menu with me, tell all she wanted us to do, and we would do our best to please her. Mrs. Harrington understood but said nothing. She just looked at me, smiled, and from that day on we made the menu and she left the kitchen and did not interfere with our work.

When my husband remarked that Mrs. Harrington did not give him so many orders at the same time anymore, I told him how I fixed that. He laughed and said, "I think Mrs. Harrington is afraid of you." But things were done and I didn't think Mrs. Harrington was ever afraid of me; I rather noticed that she was glad the way everything turned out.

Sometimes when the weather was nice, Mrs. Harrington drove to Arlington to get a few groceries, and if she went in the afternoon she took us along. We welcomed and appreciated these little outings. It meant so much to us to be able to go to the post office or see the railway station.

On other days, Mrs. Harrington said she had to be in Arlington early, and after we finished making the beds she started getting ready. She got dressed, put her hat on, and I thought she was leaving, but I noticed that she still had her slippers on. She seemed to be in a hurry but always found things to do, and it was noon before she left. Whenever after that she said she had to be early in Arlington, I was not deceived anymore. I knew that even when she had her hat on from early in the morning, as long as she had her slippers on she was not going to leave.

Another thing I thought peculiar was that the milk that the Harringtons were using which came in sealed bottles was emptied by Mrs. Harrington into a pitcher though a cheese cloth, and then the pitcher was covered with a very fine net. Also, as the weather got warmer, almost all the food, like bread, cake, scones, sugar, everything that was taken out of the cupboard, had to be covered with little covers made out of net before it was put on the table.

I wondered about these things; there were no flies or other insects around, the climate was not hot enough for that, but I guessed that Mrs. Harrington must have her reasons and I respected her wishes. In time I got so used to doing it, that long after we left Yearkerscleugh I still caught myself looking for a little net cover.

The hard work made my husband more and more hungry, and he confided in me that he could do with more substantial food. He didn't care if it was something less fancy, just as long as it would satisfy his growing appetite. One day when the butcher came, I saw in his van some canned food, and I asked Mrs. Harrington whether she would mind having canned corned beef for a change. She looked at me, not smiling, but kind of scared, and said, "Oh no. We couldn't think of eating it. In India we wouldn't have touched it." "But we are in Scotland and not in India," I said. Mrs. Harrington insisted that they would not have it, but if we fancied it, we were welcome to it. That was fine with us and my husband was happy.

Now it dawned on me why Mrs. Harrington took all those precautions like straining the milk and covering all the food. In India, these precautions were necessary and justified, but not in Scotland where it was so cold that the flies and insects had no chance of getting into the food. I could only assume that Mrs. Harrington, having lived in India for so long, could not rid herself of these habits.

Next Sunday afternoon, we went to the farm to pick up Mrs. Peters and take her for a walk. She was not quite ready yet and asked us to come to her room. The room was so small, compared with our bedroom, ours seemed like a drawing room. It was furnished with only the most necessary things, and there was no fireplace. Right now, the room was packed with Mrs. Peters's possessions. She took along all her bedding, linen, silver, dishes, sewing machine, and even her bicycle, everything that she was allowed to take out of her country. We could not visualize where she would put all her belongings unless her employers would allow her more space.

She was ready to go now, and the three of us went towards the old little village. It was a fine day, and we enjoyed the walk. And then Mrs. Peters told us her story. Under different circumstances, it would probably have taken her longer to confide in us; after all we were strangers, but our mutual misfortune made us more talkative. She was married and, as she pointed out, happily married, to a gentile for quite a few years. Her family, her parents and three brothers, all lived in the same town in Germany. They were decent, hard working people, and their only crime was their religion. When Hitler took over Germany and things went bad, Mr. Peters suggested that it would be the best thing for Mrs. Peters if she would agree to a divorce. It was, as he assured her, only a formality which would make it easier for her to get out of the country and find a job. After some time passed, he would try to go to Switzerland and then join her in England. He claimed he was very much in love with her, and it was all for her benefit. And that was how she came here.

Her family also hoped that she would be able to help them. As soon as she arrived, she wrote to committees in Glasgow asking them for advice. Her younger brother studied farming, and there was a slight possibility that he could get a visa as a farmer. But everything took time and the Nazis wouldn't wait.

We asked her what she thought of her job, and she admitted that she was in a way disappointed. When the job was offered to her, the house was described as being located on the main road, but now she found out that it was a terrible lonesome road. She was a very courageous little woman. We understood how she must have felt, but she was determined to make the best of it, as she believed that one day she would be reunited with her husband. She already had a letter from him in which he assured her of his love and faithfulness. He even wrote to her employers and thanked them for taking care of his wife.

She also told us that her hearing was not that good, and she hoped it would not interfere with her duties; and the English that she spoke was very, very poor. She was only hoping that her experience in cooking and other domestic service would make up for these shortcomings, and we assured her that they would.

It was time now to walk back to Mrs. Tandie's house, and

Mrs. Peters was glad to join us. There was an older man whom we had not met before, and he was introduced to us as Mr. Tandie's elder brother, who lived in a small town not far away from here. Mrs. Peters shook hands with everybody, as we did when we first arrived. In Central and Eastern Europe, one always shook hands with everybody when arriving and leaving. Now being almost "natives," we didn't do it anymore as we noticed the others didn't do it either, but Mrs. Peters had no opportunity of knowing it yet.

The afternoon in the Tandies' house went by so very quickly. Mr. Tandie usually joined us a little later, as he had to go over to the Harrington's house to look after the central heating. We were just sitting there talking and having tea and always some kind of little cakes. This time there was also cheese, bread, and butter. The table was covered with food, and it was offered in such a gracious and friendly manner that we could not understand why the Scotch people had the reputation of being tight. We thought of them as most generous and hospitable.

And Mrs. Tandie, seeing to it that everyone had plenty to eat and being so warm and cheerful, made it hard on us to leave. But we had to go, and Mrs. Peters shook hands with everybody again, but seeing that we didn't do it, asked us on the way home what our reason was. We were glad that she gave us the opportunity to explain, and she was grateful that we did.

We took her home and asked her if she would join us again next Sunday, but she didn't think that she would be off every Sunday, probably every other Sunday and one week day afternoon. We asked her to come and visit us on her afternoons off or after we were through with the supper; then we could sit together in our room and listen to the radio. And so the visits and walks became our mutual recreation, and the three of us got along fine.

**German Troops in Slovakia
Turning Czechs into Germans**

—*London Times*, August 20, 1939

**Congress Inquiry
Evidence of Morals at Youth Camps
Washington Correspondent**

" '. . . one item in their instruction,' she declared, 'was an explanation of the methods of sterilization necessary for all those who were Jews,' and the course included anti-racial, anti-Masonic, and anti-Christian homilies, and also pictured the future of Germany. . . .' "

—*London Times*, August 21, 1939

THE DAY ON WHICH we were to meet our friends was near, and we asked Mrs. Harrington if we could have that day off. They said that they also would go to Glasgow as they had some business to attend to, and they would make arrangements to go on the same day. They would take the train in Aylesbury so that we could drive with them to the station and in the evening back home again. At the station we parted; they took a compartment in one of the railway cars and we went into a different one. We thought it would suit everybody best and make us all feel more at ease.

After one hour travel, we arrived in Glasgow. Right from the beginning it made a different impression than Edinburgh. While Edinburgh looked like a dream with the castle and all the beautiful surroundings, Glasgow was a city of business with big office buildings and factories. But it was full of busy people and full of life, and we liked it.

We had more than an hour before our friends arrived; their train came later and left later too. We made use of the time by going to the American consul and inquiring about our immigration quota. The consul's reply was very discouraging. When he noticed where my husband was born, he said it would take many years before we would be able to go to the States.

We met our friends, and seeing them was great. Only six months were gone since we saw them in Vienna, but so many things have happened since then, and the circumstances the four of us lived in now were so different that it seemed like years. We all tried to talk at the same time; we were so anxious not to miss anything since we only had these few hours and probably would not see each other for a greater length of time.

Our discussions were mostly about our jobs, our experiences, and our mistakes. Our friends spoke and understood more English than we did, so in that respect were better off. But they didn't seem to be happy in their job. We wanted to know all about it, so Gerti told us that one of the things she resented most was that Mrs. Brown made a regular timetable of their working hours. Every minute was carefully planned for some kind of housework, except a short time in the afternoon. So that Gerti, who was usually a very quiet and sensible girl, could not help asking Mrs. Brown one day, "And what am I supposed to do if I have to go to the bathroom? There is no time provided for that in your working plan."

I laughed so hard, I could hardly stop. And when I asked her how Mrs. Brown reacted, Gerti said that she wouldn't say anything, but that things were not pleasant after that, and they were hoping to find a different job.

We went then to lunch, looked around the city, and didn't stop talking. We wanted to buy a few things and go to some different stores, but my husband was only willing to go to Woolworth's. That, he said, was the only store where he wouldn't have to talk. Should he buy something, all he had to do was hand the merchandise to the clerk, and all he had to say was "Thank you."

So Gerti and I went off by ourselves and found a tearoom where we were to meet our husbands later. The time went by fast; we only had two more hours till our train left. At three-thirty, we had coffee, not tea, talked some more, and at five our train was due to leave. Our friends saw us off, and we promised to write to each other and arrange another rendezvous. We took some pictures; I had a camera and as soon as we had these developed, we were going to send these to our friends. Finally we had to say good bye and our train left.

Mr. and Mrs. Harrington arrived on the same train and we drove home with them, already thinking of the next time we could get together again. Everything that used to be so easy back home and was taken for granted, like meeting our friends, now took on such a different and important meaning.

A few weeks later, we heard from our friends that they left their job and accepted one in a different town and were well satisfied. They were going to tell us all about it as soon as we met again.

The last two weeks in June were beautiful. Not one rainy day, sunshine all the time, just lovely. And Mr. Tandie had to say each time, "grand day."

The Harringtons drove out more often now. Mr. Harrington was very fond of fish, so they went to Arlington and bought haddock and kippers for breakfast. We didn't like haddock at all. Mrs. Harrington told me to cook it in milk to take the dryness away, but we still didn't like it.

We enjoyed the hours when the Harringtons were gone; we had more free time and could sit in the now so green and beautiful garden. What was still puzzling us however was why the hills around us remained bare except that instead of being yellow, they were green and why nothing was growing on that spacious land. We decided once more to ask the Tandies.

On Sunday then, we asked them and were told that what we called hills were really called moors and that the land was really only good for raising sheep, and corn wouldn't grow. We didn't know what moors were and had to look it up in our dictionary. And when we found out what it meant, we understood why there would be no vegetation. But not all the moors were so bare. On one of them was a lovely little tree and higher up grew some pretty pink-colored something that we learned to know as heather.

After June was over, the beautiful weather seemed to come to an end too. We had more rain and less sunshine, and Mr. Tandie could again take his pick in describing each morning. We complained to Mrs. Tandie about the weather; now that we expected the days to be warm and beautiful, it was chilly and rainy. "Well," she said, "That's Scotland for you." And went around working and whistling.

In the back of the garden behind the well-kept grounds, there was a kitchen garden where Mr. Tandie tried to grow a few vegetables and some raspberries. (I say he tried, because in that cold and damp climate it was a hard job to make anything grow. There were some cherry trees, but we have never seen a cherry on the trees.)

We were surprised to see that Mr. Tandie had the vegetable beds and the raspberries covered with heavy nets. We asked him why he had to do that, and he told us that the rabbits were so numerous and got into everything that was edible and, if he didn't cover it up, they would ruin everything over night.

It was hard to believe that these little animals, who were our only company when we took our walks, would do a thing like that, and we told Mr. Tandie so. But he laughed and assured us that this is what they do, and in order to prevent it, it would even be necessary to get rid of them. When we asked him how he would go about it, he said, "We shoot them."

"Do you like rabbit meat?" he asked, almost at the same time. I said we had never tasted it; we didn't know one eats that kind of meat, and Mr. Tandie said we should try it someday, it tasted real good. My husband didn't say anything.

"The raspberries will grow big and juicy this summer because of the rain we're having," said Mr. Tandie. And they tasted wonderful. We knew that as we also had raspberries in our country and I liked them very much.

On our way home, my husband finally said, "How in the world

could one eat rabbits, these little things running around; I can't even think about it. Could you?" he asked. I said that I wouldn't know; I never thought about it that way. After all, chickens run around too and we eat them. The answer my husband gave me was, "We don't see chickens running around like rabbits, we only see them when they are ready to eat."

When the raspberries were ripe, big and juicy like Mr. Tandie prophesied, Mrs. Harrington liked them served on top of rice pudding. They were very tasty and much better than we had ever eaten before. As there was plenty of them, we had rice pudding every night as long as they lasted, and they lasted a long time. I didn't mind; I liked rice pudding, but when the raspberries were gone, my husband said he would never again even look at rice pudding.

Up to now, we never had any visitors and got resigned to the quiet life that the Harringtons seemed to prefer. But one day Mrs. Harrington announced that she was expecting Lady Stalward for tea. Mrs. Harrington must have thought a lot of that lady because she was very anxious that everything go according to the rules. She gave my husband all kinds of instructions like: to help her ladyship out of the car, to open the door for her and lead her into the dining room. Lady Stalward was an old lady; she carried a cane, and her chauffeur helped her out of the car. Apart from that, she didn't want any help; she passed my husband, went into the house with no fuss whatever.

The chauffeur had tea with us and, though it was difficult to make conversation, we did understand that her Ladyship came from a very old and distinguished family. After tea Mr. Harrington was showing Lady Stalward the grounds. In spite of her age and the cane, she could move around easily and walk a great deal. She seemed to like the place and seemed to have fun, because we heard them laughing and chatting. Soon came the visit to the end and with it all the excitement.

A few weeks later we had another visit; this time the Harringtons expected the employers of Mrs. Peters who owned the farm, and they were to come after supper. Before they came, my husband got instruction again. He was to take Mrs. Galloway's wrap, she was expected to go to the cloak room, and he was supposed to wait for her and show her into the morning room where Mrs. Harrington was to pour the coffee and he was to serve it.

The couple arrived and with them the young man we saw minding the sheep. We were surprised to see him; we thought he just worked for them. But our good Tandies informed us later that he owned a part of the farm.

Well, everything turned out different as expected. Mrs. Galloway wouldn't take off her wrap; even when my husband tried to take it from her, she held onto it. She didn't go into the cloak room either; she just joined the two men and went straight into the morning room. There was nothing more for my husband to do but follow them and serve the coffee.

There were no more visits for the moment, and no more excitement. Now and then, my husband seemed to get tired of cleaning and dusting but didn't complain too much. Once he came into the kitchen looking lost in his thoughts, and I wanted to know what was wrong. Did he by any chance break some glasses or Mr. Harrington's whiskey bottle. He said it was something else that was bothering him, something peculiar has happened.

All of a sudden the work he was doing seemed so monotonous that he felt he had to do something different. As there was not much he could do, he wanted to play a little joke just to get away from the daily routine. I could hardly wait to know what the joke was, and so he told me:

"You know that my two favorite pictures of the Harrington's ancestors were the two I named Lady Sarah and Sir Lancy. My joke was that I swept the dust under the rug instead of into the dust pan. I don't really know why I did that. I guess because I was bored; I soon was convinced that it was silly when I happened to look up at Lady Sarah's picture and had this feeling that she gave me a disgusting look as if I had committed a crime. And I was almost ready to do the right thing when I glanced at Sir Lancy and noticed a twinkle in his eye as if he would say, 'Leave it there, old boy, and let's see what happens.' And then it happened," my husband continued. "Mrs. Harrington came into the room, lifted the rug, took the sweeper out of my hand, swept the dust back into the middle of the room, gave the sweeper back to me, smiled and left the room."

"Did you say anything to Mrs. Harrington?" I asked. "There was no time to utter a single word; she was out as fast as she came in. I gave Sir Lancy an angry look and went on with my work."

"Never mind your fantasy with Lady Sarah and Sir Lancy, how did Mrs. Harrington know?"

"That's what bothers me, how did she know unless she had a telepathic connection with the dead?"

"But those are not even Mrs. Harrington's ancestors," I said, joining my husband in his imagination, but I was convinced that there was a very simple explanation. And so we had our little jokes and built our own world around the castle of Yearkescleugh.

The big black range in the kitchen was to be replaced with a modern one. Four men arrived one morning to dismantle the old coal range which gave me such a bad time when we first arrived. Mrs. Harrington ordered an Aga Cooker. Now that we had to part with it, I got sentimental about it. It wasn't quite as bad as it looked, and, though I never polished it since it was so beautifully cleaned by Mrs. Tandie, it still kept its shine. The men stayed with the Tandies; I just had to make tea for them a few times a day. All the other meals they took at the Tandies' house.

After a few days' work, there stood an elegant-looking range built entirely of ivory tiles. It was as big as the old one, had no open fire, and was heated with anthracite and had to be kept going all the time. My husband had to feed it twice a day. In order to operate it, I had to study a special booklet. There were divisions for keeping the dishes warm, for making porridge, for steaming puddings, and so on. Porridge was prepared the night before, and by morning it was thick and creamy and it tasted good. The first time we put it in the wrong place, and by morning it was all burned. Puddings just took a certain time; one didn't even have to watch them. The same applied to a roast or a leg of lamb. On top of the Aga Cooker were two large flat plates, one for very fast cooking, the other for slow. After a while, I got used to it and it was easy to handle and easy to keep clean.

One early morning, soon after we came down and got ready to prepare breakfast, we heard a lorry arrive and soon there was a knock on the front door. My husband opened the door and a man stood there, said "Nice day," and handed him a package. He then turned around and went back to the lorry where he talked to two more men, and they started to unload some tools.

We assumed that Mrs. Harrington wanted to have some work done and just didn't mention it to us. She must have heard the commotion because she came downstairs and asked us what was going on. We told her that there were some men outside, apparently here to do some work, and my husband asked her what to do with the little package. Mrs. Harrington opened it and we saw that it contained loose tea mixed with sugar. She took it, went to the door, called the man to come over as she wanted to talk to him. When the man came over she said a few words to him and gave him his tea back; the man then returned to the lorry, told the man to put the tools back again, and they drove off.

Mrs. Harrington explained to us that there was a mistake; she didn't order anyone to come; they were probably to work someplace else. She didn't explain anything about the tea and went back upstairs. But we were curious why the men brought tea and then took it back with them again; it was something that the Tandies would have to explain again.

The answer was very simple, only to us these things looked so mysterious. Mrs. Tandie said that the men brought tea with them because they were expecting to work all day and wanted tea with their lunch which they carried with them to work. They wanted us to brew it for them and supply them with plenty of hot water. "Why," she asked, "don't people do it the same way where you come from? After all there are no inns or pubs around here where they could get anything to drink."

We told her we wouldn't know what people did in the country in Austria, but one thing was sure, they wouldn't carry tea around with them; they probably expected the people they worked for to provide them with lunch and beer. We were hoping that Mrs. Tandie would not think us a nuisance asking all these questions, and we told her so. But she assured us that she enjoyed to answer all we wanted to know and we should feel free to ask. It showed how different our countries were; she was only sorry that we knew so very little about each other.

In the kitchen garden grew blackberries which tasted delicious, and we all liked to eat them. One afternoon, it happened to be a sunny day, we went out to pick some of them. Mr. Harrington was there too and was showing us the bushes where they grew, when we noticed someone coming out of the house, covered almost from top to bottom with a kind of net and wearing gloves. We looked up and Mr. Harrington said, "Oh, that's Mrs. Harrington" and called out to her to join him. I was so flabbergasted, I just stood there staring and thinking, "Why in the world is she covered up like that?" My first thought was that she was afraid of the sun, but the sun was never so hot in this part of the country that one could even obtain a slight sun tan. So what could it be? And then it came to me in a flash: "India and the flies." That was it, and that was what Mrs. Harrington was afraid of. When I caught myself still staring at her, I realized I must not do it if I didn't want to embarrass her. But Mrs. Harrington was not in the least embarrassed. She went around the garden as if it was the most common thing in the world to pick berries looking like a bride.

Whenever the Harringtons went out for a ride, they were usually home before dark. That day they were late, and when they finally arrived, Mrs. Harrington said the ride took them longer than they expected and then coming home they had a little accident. Just before turning into the gate, a rabbit ran into the car, and, before they could stop, the poor thing was hit.

Mr. Tandie seeing the car stop, came out of his cottage, and, when he saw the dead rabbit, he said he would take the skin off, clean, and hang it up in the back of the scullery for a few days, after which the rabbit could be cooked and make a delicious meal. But Mrs. Harrington, telling us all, remarked that neither she nor Mr. Harrington were fond of rabbit, but the two of us might like it. Right then and there we should have told her how we feel about eating rabbits. Instead, I looked at my husband, and noticing how bewildered and at the same time funny his expression was, I had to turn away not to burst out laughing. And then it was too late. Mrs. Harrington, being in a hurry, didn't wait for our opinion, but left the kitchen. But even so, I don't think we would have told her, because she would not have understood. "Well," I said to my husband, "we will have to eat rabbit, and who knows we might even like it." "Oh, no, not me," he said. "It makes me sick to think about it, and if I knew I won't get anything to eat that day, I will not eat that poor animal." "So are you going to tell Mrs. Harrington?" I asked. "I will think of something; I just have to."

Three days later, when it was almost time for the rabbit to be cooked, my husband went through the kitchen towards the back of the scullery. When I asked him where he was going in the middle of dusting the dining room, he said that he will be back soon and tell me. About 20 minutes later he came back and said: "I buried the rabbit." When I thought I didn't hear right, he repeated, "I tell you I buried the rabbit." I must have still looked stupefied because he tried to explain. When he told me that he would have to think of some excuse in order to avoid eating it, he had no idea what kind of excuse he would use. And then he remembered how Mrs. Harrington came out in the garden the other day, all covered up, and he finally had a brain wave. He told her he noticed a few flies around the rabbit, and that the meat didn't look too inviting. That did it; she ordered him to bury the rabbit in the furthest corner of the kitchen garden.

I laughed so hard, I was afraid the Harringtons might hear me and tried to stop. When I finally did, I said, "That was a mean thing to do, to take advantage of Mrs. Harrington's fear of flies." "I know," he said, "but I was desperate, and it was only a white lie and seemed the only sensible way out, and nobody was hurt."

I don't really know whether Mrs. Harrington, after thinking about it or maybe telling it to the Tandies, ever believed the story. Anyway nothing was said anymore, and the Tandies never asked how we liked the rabbit, and we were very grateful that they didn't.

Though Mr. Harrington didn't care for rabbit, he was fond of hare soup. Mrs. Tandie was the only one who knew how to prepare it. She came over and cooked the hare for hours in its own blood; after it was ready cooked and was all red, she took the meat out and only the soup was eaten. I had to taste it because I was curious, but could not really eat it. All that blood made me almost sick, and my husband gave me a look full of contempt.

Pat, Mrs. Harrington's little granddaughter, arrived early in July to spend some of her vacation with us. She is about six years old, a very pretty and well-behaved child. To her we must have seemed very strange. She had never heard anybody talk like we did. Sometimes she sat very quietly in the kitchen next to Mrs. Harrington when she prepared the menu for the day, looked at me, and just listened. She didn't like the weather; it rained everyday. One day when she was quite annoyed with the barometer falling all the time, she hit it so that the temperature would go up; but it didn't help, it went on raining.

One week later Miss Ida arrived; she is Mrs. Harrington's youngest sister. She is a teacher (Mrs. Tandie informed us) and is a very pleasant person. She loved to go out in the woods, walking there for hours, rain or no rain. Every morning after breakfast, she walked through the pantry where I washed the dishes, and I always said good morning to her. At first she looked at me a little amazed, but said good morning also, took her basket with her tools and went out gardening. We liked Miss Ida and Pat; they brought a little more life into the house.

The next time we met our friends was already the end of July. Mr. and Mrs. Harrington were driving to Sterling and suggested that we meet our friends there. They agreed gladly, and so we went to Sterling. It was a nice day. We met early and had almost a whole day to ourselves. The first thing we wanted was to talk. We found a nice little place, had breakfast, and talked about everything. Back home we were used to discussing all kinds of problems, politics, work, theater, and we missed that way of life very much. Now that we were here together with people who have the same background, we were eager not to lose a moment of the precious time.

After we had talked about the whole world, we thought we had better look around Sterling. It is an old and very interesting town.

There is a castle with a history of a few hundred years and an old cemetery. It started to rain, and we had to take refuge in a little restaurant again. By now it was time for lunch, and our friends still had to tell us about their new job.

They liked it much better; Gerti did not have such a strict schedule as in her previous job; to the contrary, she could arrange her work anyway she wanted. Also the household seemed to be on the more generous side; the people were more easy going. Oscar accompanied his employer on fishing trips; they had quite a few more visitors, so they had a more lively time.

Still Oscar could not get used to the daily cleaning and dusting routine; he often got very impatient, and, with   ng that was going on in the world, this work seemed so very unimportant. He said he was not sure how long he would be able to keep up with that kind of a job in the country where one hardly knew what was going on. We all felt the same way, but there was no place we could go. We just had to stick it out and be glad that we had some kind of a home. We had to leave now, to meet Mr. and Mrs. Harrington and drive back with them. We said "Auf Wiedersehen" hoping to see them again in the early fall.

The news we received from home was very sad. Our relations had lost their apartment and had to move in with some strange family and all squeeze into two tiny rooms. They lived under a terrific tension, threatened to be sent away to some unknown destination. And we were not able to help them. The committees had so many early applications on their hands, they could not even cope with these.

We decided to talk to Mrs. Harrington and ask her advice. She said she would talk it over with Mr. Harrington, and they suggested we should put an ad in the Glasgow paper, looking for a job in a household that could employ a mother and a daughter. It was my husband's mother and sister. Mrs. Harrington was very understanding; she offered to send the ad in, also saying that whoever was interested should contact her.

Miss Ida and Pat were still with us, Miss Ida still gardening and Pat still playing with her toys. She had no play mates around and got quite bored at times. Out in the woods was a tennis court, somewhat neglected but still quite usable. Mrs. Harrington asked my husband one afternoon — it stopped raining — to play tennis with Pat. He never did before, but Mrs. Harrington said that didn't matter as long as Pat could be busy for a while.

I thought, I have to see that, and went out to watch them. I wondered how those two would get along. Both were not dressed according to the rules; my husband wore a dark suit, and Pat a coat as it was cold and damp. To my surprise they had fun. They played and laughed, and the language was no obstacle.

Beginning of August, Miss Ida and Pat left, and we were sorry to see them go. Both were so very pleasant. Miss Ida was very generous; she left us a nice tip, the first we had ever received.

Ten days had passed since we put an ad in the paper, and so far there was no response. But on our next Sunday off, we were walking toward Mrs. Peters's house. We intended to pick her up, when we saw a black car stopping in front of us. A middle-aged woman stepped out and asked if we were Mr. and Mrs. Schneider. She told us she came with her mother because of the ad, and, as the old lady could not get out of the car because of her bad leg, she wondered if we could take them to Mrs. Harrington.

We were very happy to and drove with them to the house. I was so excited and ran up to ask Mrs. Harrington to come down and talk to them. She did so immediately, joined them in the car, and, while we waited outside being very nervous about the outcome of their conversation, they talked a long time. Then Mrs. Harrington came out of the car, and the old lady asked us how we liked it here. We replied that we liked it very much, and she said she would let us know what they decided, and they drove off.

One week later, we received a letter and were notified by the daughter that they were willing to take the necessary steps in order to obtain the domestic permit. Right away we wrote to my husband's family telling them about the job and asking them to inquire what preparations they could make over there to speed up their coming. We knew that it would take quite a while for the permit to come through; we remembered how long we had to wait, but at the same time we were hoping for a speedier procedure as the job was already secured.

We listened to the wireless every available moment. Hitler boasted about the war, and the days went by, and the permit was still to come. How we waited every day, but only we and our loved ones were in a hurry. The permit had to go the usual way, and then it was too late.

Though Mr. Harrington kept saying there will be no war, he was still very optimistic; I was the first one in Yearkerscleugh to receive the bad news. When on the first of September I waited for the baker to deliver the bread, he told me the terrible news. The Germans started to bomb Warsaw, and the war was on.

Letters to the Editor:

"Sir, — The attitude of The Times and of humanely disposed people generally towards the Jewish refugee question is wrong. . . . We should stand up to Nazi Germany in a cold and practical manner. In this way we shall be able to render better service to the suffering Jews." Robert P. Skinner
— *London Times,* August 22, 1939

Invasion of Poland
Germans Attack Across All Frontiers
Warsaw and Other Cities Bombed
British Obligations Will Be Fulfilled

— *London Times,* September 2, 1939

The Children Move Off
Evacuation of 500,000

— *London Times,* September 2, 1939

Britain's Fight to Save the World
Unity in Both Houses, Complete Powers for the Government

— *London Times,* September 4, 1939

At War With Germany
Britain and France Take Up the Challenge

— *London Times,* September 4, 1939

Plays for Evacuated Children
Suggested Formation of Touring Companies

— *London Times,* September 7, 1939

~ 8 ~

MRS. HARRINGTON didn't smile at all that day. All she said was, "Mr. Harrington was wrong." Now all our hopes to get our family over were shattered. We were completely cut off from our country and had no way of knowing what was happening over there. There was no more talk about Pat's parents coming home from India; things looked as if they would not come home until after the war.

Poor Mrs. Peters, all her hopes of being reunited with her husband again or to be able to help her family were gone too. And she was so alone. We were at least together and could talk about our worries, but she had no one. We tried to be with her as much as we could; on her week days off she went to Mrs. Tandie in the afternoon, and after supper came to our place. We spent a few hours together and then took her home.

Around us, on the surface, nothing changed except that the windows in the rooms that were in use had to be blacked out. On the first evening, Mr. and Mrs. Harrington went around the house to check that not a streak of light would come through. But on one occasion (we went for a walk in the evening), Mrs. Harrington went in one of the rooms that had to be blacked out. We saw a bright light that illuminated the whole front of the castle and the adjoining grounds. Luckily enough it wasn't noticed by anybody; we were so far into the country that, at the beginning of the war, it didn't matter.

Food was still plentiful, but once in a while Mrs. Harrington got panicky and bought huge quantities of rice, semolina, and maize flour which we never used. Mr. Harrington liked rice, but he liked it the way they cooked it in India. I had to depend on Mrs. Harrington's instructions here; they must have had a differ-

most important thing was that the cottage where the Tandies lived was so close and we could move around freely in these places.

Unpleasant as these events must have been for our employers, they never made any remarks, and things eventually calmed down. The cooking and cleaning went on as usual. Still, there seemed to be a slight change in the behavior of the Harringtons towards us. To an outsider, it would not have been noticeable, but we felt that everything was not as it used to be only a short time ago. One of the things we thought to notice was that Mr. Harrington, who was, if not talkative, always friendly, but now seemed to avoid looking at us. Mrs. Harrington continued to smile, but her smile was somehow artificial.

We could not explain what went wrong but we both felt that the atmosphere which prevailed before was gone. It was not possible for us to ask the Harringtons what, if anything, they had against us; there was nothing we could put a finger on, and so we told ourselves and hoped that all was imagination on our part caused by the excitement and happenings of the last few days.

But it was not imagination. Something was wrong. We got the explanation in a rather peculiar way because it came from London. We had a friend there who also was a domestic servant and had the opportunity to get together with other refugees in a club where quite a number of them met. She then wrote to us that, as soon as the war broke out, many of the girls who came over on the same permit as she and we did, were immediately dismissed from their jobs. Their employers turned against them because they came from countries that caused the war, not realizing that they actually persecuted the persecuted.

And that must have also been the reason why the Harringtons acted the way they did. It made us feel very sad. Though we did not for one moment believe that our employers would do the same to us as was done in London to the refugee girls, if we had a place to go to we might have left. We were hoping that when our time came to appear before the tribunal and we, as we surely would, would be declared as loyal to our new country, the attitude of Mr. and Mrs. Harrington toward us would change.

Heavy Fighting in Poland
Germans Claim Cracow

— London Times, September 7, 1939

Fair Sharing of Food
No Scarcity Implied

— London Times, September 9, 1939

Poland's Gallant Struggle
Army Intact and Sprit Unbroken

— London Times, September 11, 1939

Hungarian Servants

To the Editor of The Times:
"Sir,— It has come to my knowledge that many British employers on the outbreak of war summarily dismissed their Hungarian maids without even paying them the week's wages legally due to them. . . ." Ethel Snowden
— London Times, September 12, 1939

To the Editor of The Times:
"Sir,— In our district we were expecting school children and mothers with infants. Cots were dug out of attics, high chairs prepared, and toys collected for the amusement of the little ones. At the last moment something went wrong, and instead of little children, 500 secondary school boys of from 15 to 18 descended on the district. . . ."
— London Times, September 12, 1939

British Troops in France
Fighting in Large Numbers
German Halt Before Warsaw
Poles Breaking Through Enemy Ring

— London Times, September 12, 1939

~ 9 ~

WITH GREAT JOY we noticed that the Tandies didn't change. On the contrary, they were closer to us and more understanding. They tried to cheer us up, and Mrs. Tandie prepared the high tea with even more care and good things than before. She kept saying we shouldn't worry, and, when we sat together and talked about the war, we all were hopeful that it wouldn't last long, and there was never any doubt in our minds that the Allied powers would win.

One morning when my husband went down to the cellar, as he did every morning, I heard him talking to Mrs. Tandie. I wondered what happened to Mr. Tandie; he usually looked after the central heating, and it was the first time Mrs. Tandie came instead. When my husband and Mrs. Tandie came up from the scullery, I saw my husband smiling and saying something I could not hear. I then asked her where Mr. Tandie was, if anything was wrong with him. When I heard from her the news, I said I was sorry, and we talked for a while; then she left.

My husband, who was watching us, asked me now, "Why did you look so grave at Mrs. Tandie and say you were sorry? Did you hurt her feelings in any way and had to apologize? She is always so good to us." I looked at him flabbergasted. "Why should I have hurt Mrs. Tandie's feelings? I didn't apologize to her; I didn't have any reason," I said. "But you said you were sorry." "What was I supposed to say, when she told me that Mr. Tandie's brother died, and that Mr. Tandie went to the funeral?" Now it was my husband's turn to look flabbergasted. "Oh no," he said, and I told her, "It's nice for a change." "What is nice for a change, what are you talking about?"

And so it all came out. All he understood was that Mr. Tandie had gone to Lymington to see his brother; that part about the funeral he didn't get. He had heard the expression "nice for a change" from Mr. Tandie and thought now is the proper time to use it.

We couldn't help it, we had to laugh. These mistakes were really too much. He wanted to run after Mrs. Tandie and tell her how sorry he was, but I told him not to do it; she must have realized by now that it was a mistake and might be laughing now also.

Feeling still embarrassed, my husband only reluctantly agreed to visit the Tandies that coming Sunday. I knew they were expecting us and convinced him that he was exaggerating the whole matter, and we went to their house. They were just as warm and hospitable as always; Mrs. Tandie even made a little surprise for us. She prepared little individual meat pies which we enjoyed very much, and we told her so. And then she, looking at us with her charming sile, said, "I was hoping you would like them; they're nice for a change." With these few words, she made my husband feel so much better; we all laughed and had a wonderful afternoon.

By the end of September, I had a little accident: one of my teeth broke and as it was visible, I felt very conscious about it. There was no dentist in the neighborhood who could replace my tooth. In order to have it done properly, we had to go to Glasgow. We got in touch with our friends, asking if we could meet them again, but it was not possible for them to come at that time.

We had to apply for a permit, and Mrs. Harrington helped us do so; a few days later the permit arrived. As the Harringtons did not take us to the station, we had to walk. And, as we wanted to make the early trian, we had to start out from Yearkerscleugh about six o'clock in the morning. I couldn't have walked all that distance in my walking shoes and had to put on the ones I used to climb mountains with in Austria. The walking shoes I took along and changed them at the station. The station master was nice about it, allowed me to leave the heavy ones there until evening, when I had to repeat the procedure again.

The first thing we had to do in Glasgow was to find a dentist. We went to the refugee committee and were given an address of a dentist who was also a refugee from Germany. As I did not have an appointment, we had to wait for quite some time. He must have come to Glasgow soon after Hitler took over, because he seemed to be well-established and settled. People who left right in 1933 were better off; they could take along most of their belongings and even some money.

He looked at my tooth and told me that I would have to come back at least three times. I explained the situation to him and told him that the best I could do was to come back in four weeks. That was all right with him; I should just let him know the days so he could expect me. We were glad that our friends didn't come; we would have had very little time together. We could only window shop for a little while, have a bite to eat, and then it was time to take the train home.

At the station in Arlington after I changed my shoes, the station master asked if we had a pleasant day. We said we did, but it wasn't quite true. Now that the war was on, one could feel the tension that weighed upon the people and the whole town. Whoever could was trying to rush home before dark, as there were no lights whatsoever in the streets. We had to carry a torch (flashlight), and it was hard to imagine an entire city like Glasgow entirely blacked out. It was still daylight when we left, and in the country we never had any street lights anyway.

As the war went on, announcements were made over the wireless that a certain amount of families with children would have to be evacuated from the larger cities into the country. People with available space were asked to take the families, at least for the time being, until it was made certain that the evacuees would be safe to return home.

There was plenty of room in the "big house," and Mrs. Tandie told us that the Harringtons would probably make some of it available to a family with children, and soon afterwards Mrs. Harrington told us that they had decided to do so. At the same time, she asked if we wouldn't mind to give up our sitting room as it had two smaller adjoining rooms which could be used as bedrooms for the family. We of course didn't mind; we just took the little radio into our bedroom and listened to it there.

Mrs. Harrington got busy. She ordered six iron beds, pillows, blankets, sheets, and pillowcases, and even some chests of drawers. The rooms were scrubbed, windows washed, and, when the beds arrived, Mr. Tandie came over to help put them up. Mrs. Harrington worried whether six beds would be sufficient, but Mr. Tandie assured her that the family who was coming was not used to much comfort. Some of the children didn't even have a bed, and they would be happy to sleep two in one bed. I wondered what kind of evacuees we would be getting.

Into the scullery adjoining the rooms, Mrs. Harrington had an oil stove put in. She also brought in pots and pans, all kinds of dishes; there was a regular little household installed. She wanted the family to be quite independent of the rest of the house, and I must say she did everything to make them feel comfortable.

And then they arrived. Mr. Harrington went to the station to pick them up and brought a car load of children and their mother back with him. While they were getting out of the car, he looked at us and at them and shrugged his shoulders and whispered, "They will be going home soon, in a few days, it won't last long." I don't know, did he mean the war or the refugees woouldn't last long? In any case, he was wrong once more.

Here they were now, six children and their mother, Mrs. Hill. Mr. Hill was left in Glasgow; we thought that his work must keep him there. The children, though one could see that the family was poor, were lovely children, three girls and three boys; two of the boys, the youngest, were twins. The oldest girl was about fourteen years old; the others were each one year younger; only the twins were about four years old. They were all very shy. Mrs. Hill looked quite sad, but seemed a nice perosn.

They were shown into their rooms. Mrs. Tandie came over to talk with them and make them feel at ease. She explained to Mrs. Hill how the oil stove worked and told her also that she can buy her food from the butcher, the baker, and the fruit man who came to the house. They had hardly any luggage. I wondered if their luggage might arrive later but it didn't.

The children were very quiet and well behaved as if they were afraid to make any noise. Now and then we could see them playing in the back garden, but they were very anxious not to disturb anybody. As the days went by, their pale cheeks got a little more color, and they seemed very happy.

We would have liked to talk to them or to their mother but we could not understand what they were saying. Glasgow seemed to have a slang of its own, and they, of course, had a hard time to make out what we were saying. So all we could do was smile at each other.

Mrs. Tandie made friends with the children, and one day brought home a tiny, black kitten so that the children could have a pet. The kitten took a fancy to Mrs. Hill, and it followed her around, and, when it ran outside of the garden, she was the only one who could make it come back. It was such a sweet little thing that we also grew fond of it. Mrs. Harrington didn't like cats, and Sheila was jealous, so the kitten had to be kept in the back of the house.

Soon we noticed that all Mrs. Hill cooked for her family were sausages or ready-bought pies which she only had to warm up, and she used drippings with everything. There was a very unpleasant smell through the house all the time. I was sorry for Mrs. Harrington; her smile now took on a sad look. As she never complained or expressed her feelings in any way, we got used to watch[ing] her smile. She probably never knew how much her smile could tell us.

We saw one day that the rooms the Hill family occupied did not look as clean anymore as when they arrived. As a matter of fact, they looked bad. The beds were never made, the walls showed all the finger marks, the oil stove was full of grease, and the dishes were seldom washed. All that and the smell made us feel miserable, and Mrs. Harrington must have been going through an ordeal.

One Sunday afternoon, I told Mrs. Tandie about it and asked her what kind of a woman Mrs. Hill was that she did not care how her family lived but always had time to put here hair in curls. After all, they must have had some sort of home in Glasgow too. I also asked her what Mr. Hill was doing. Mrs. Tandie then told us that Mrs. Hill came from a Glasgow slum. Mr. Hill was unemployed for years; he didn't seem to be fond of work, and, as by law, he could not be forced to take any kind of job that was available, only a job he thought was in his line. He rather had all these children and drew unemployment compensation for all of them. Mrs. Hill never had a decent place in her life; all eight of them occupied one room, she never had a proper kitchen, and never learned to keep house. She was a good-hearted woman, modest and quiet, and if she would have had the opportunity, and if her husband wanted to work, things might have looked different. We all felt sorry for the children; what kind of life were they offered? When the older children had to go to school, Mrs. Harrington saw to it that they had boots, warm scarves and gloves, The Harringtons were indeed very generous toward the Hill family.

The four weeks were over, and I had to see my dentist again. This time our friends were able to join us, and as I had made an appointment with my dentist, we would have more time to spend with them. They also had to apply for a permit, so we had to plan carefully and try to get the permit for that specific day.

But as always the more anxious one is to have things in time, these things go wrong. The permit, which was supposed to arrive one day before our trip, did not come. We didn't know what to do. I had to see the dentist, and our friends were coming too, and here we were stranded. We asked Mrs. Harrington what if anything could be done, and she had an idea that might be of help. There was another mail coming in the afternoon, but it wouldn't be delivered to us until the next morning, too late for us to catch the train. There was a chance that the permit would arrive with the afternoon mail. Mrs. Harrington called the post office in Arlington and asked the clerk to notify the constable should the permit arrive. And then she called the constable, who had to put his stamp on the permit, [to ask] if he would let her know when the permit was here, and he was even willing to pick it up from the post office and notify her. Later, almost in the evening, came a call from the constable; the permit had arrived and he would have it all ready for us to pick up in his house before we went to the train. It would be quite early in the morning, but he didn't mind.

It was still dark the next day when we started for Arlington. I in my heavy shoes, carrying the other pair under my arm, we went straight to the constable's house. His wife was up, and she handed us a cup of tea; then he came out still quite sleepy and handed us the permit. When we told him how sorry we were to cause all that trouble, he said we shouldn't worry and wished us a pleasant day. What friendly sort of people they were.

We met our friends, and to see them again was great. There was a lot to talk about now that the war was on. They also worried so much about their families being still in Austria. They didn't experience that change of attitude on the part of their employers that we did; their job was fine, and they were waiting to appear before the tribunal. Oscar was even more impatient now. He thought it was ridiculous to have to be busy with cooking and cleaning when more important things were happening in the world. But Gerti was the more sensible one. She tried to make him see that they couldn't help end the war by leaving their job.

While I was at the dentist, the three of them took a stroll around the city. Later we met and had lunch together. We talked some more, walked again, and as we did so we noticed a big sign that said, "Don't fight for England."

All four of us were quite taken aback and could not figure out what that sign was supposed to mean. We decided that, as soon as we got home, we would ask the Tandies, and they were going to ask their employers. We bought some chocolates and biscuits, which we were going to take to Mrs. Tandie, and had to say good bye to our friends again.

After we arrived home, we went to the Tandies' house, as we knew that they would expect us and have tea ready for us. That sign in Glasgow bothered my husband, and, as soon as we sat down, he asked Mr. Tandie to explain it to him. Mr. Tandie looked at Mrs. Tandie. And they both smiled and he said, "We don't fight for England, we fight for Britain."

Mrs. Tandie let us in on a little secret. Mrs. Harrington confided in her that she would like to have the Hill family a little farther away. She assured her that she wouldn't want them to leave as long as they wouldn't be safe in their home in Glasgow, but they might be better off if they had a little place all to themselves. Also for the children, it would be so much nicer to have a part of the garden where they could play and run around more freely.

We all knew how Mrs. Harrington felt; she put up a brave fight until now, having all that smell under her nose. We wondered where they could go. Mrs. Tandie said there was a nice little cottage in the back of the kitchen garden which hadn't been used in years, but Mrs. Harrington would have it fixed up so that the Hills could have a proper place to stay. There was also a bathroom where the children could get a good scrubbing. Not that in the other place they couldn't keep clean; near the scullery was a wash house where, if Mrs. Hill would have taken the trouble, the children could have been just as neat and clean looking as if they had a bathroom.

Soon Mrs. Harrington informed us about her plan. She had everybody working on that cottage; a carpenter was called in to fix the window frames, and the Tandies and my husband scrubbed the floors and whitewashed the walls. All the beds were moved into the cottage, the bathroom was all white, the kitchen range was polished, coal was in the cellar, all the Hills had to do was walk in.

They were really lucky to have come to people like the Harringtons. Very few people would have gone to such trouble and expense for a family they hardly knew. We all had the same thoughts; we all hoped that Mrs. Hill, who, by now, was able to see how Mrs. Tandie kept her house and also got to know some parts of the "big house" would learn a lesson and apply it to her new place.

Mr. Hill came to spend the weekend with his family. He seemed to improve with change and the comfort and walked around as if the whole estate would belong to him. And so they stayed there, as it seemed quite happy, especially the children, who, as the weather was still pleasant, enjoyed the garden. None of us interfered with the family; for the time being we all thought it best not to visit with them until a later date when they were properly settled.

We kept on seeing Mrs. Peters who was at times quite depressed. Her employers did not take any evacuees in. The place was not big enough for an additional family, and for Mrs. Peters's sake we were glad that they didn't. She worked so hard anyway; besides the cooking and cleaning she also had all the washing to do by hand. She never complained and did all that was asked of her and did it so well and skillfully.

On one of her free Sunday afternoons, we went to pick her up for a walk. She usually waited for us at the front door, but this time she was not there. When we went into the house wondering what has happened, we heard her calling and asking us to come up into her tiny room. She was in bed and said she was so tired she could not right then go for a walk but she will try and join us later. Something in her behavior made us ask if there was anything wrong. At first she hesitated with her answer, but after a while she admitted that there was; she had some difficulties with her lady. When she applied for her job still in Germany, she didn't mention that she couldn't hear very well. She thought of it as such a slight handicap that it would not be noticeable, and she was afraid, should she mention it, of not being hired. Now her employers noticed it because, once or twice, when the doorbell rang, Mrs. Peters couldn't hear it, and Mrs. Galloway had to go to the door herself, which she resented and let Mrs. Peters know. But Mrs. Peters thought that her hearing must have gotten worse, maybe because of the many worries she had, and seemed very upset.

We were quite annoyed with Mrs. Galloway. There were not that many callers in that lonely place that it mattered so much. And what telling about the hard hearing on the part of Mrs. Peters concerned, Mrs. Galloway didn't make it clear what a lonely place her farm was. On the contrary, she wrote to her that it was on a main road, but what a deserted main road she didn't say. And where would she find such a wonderful worker? Didn't that make up for not hearing the doorbell ring?

We tried to comfort Mrs. Peters and told her not to worry and get all upset. We had plenty of other more important things to worry about. We told her too that her employers should consider themselves lucky to have Mrs. Peters working for them. She thought we were right and promised to get hold of herself. She asked us to walk to the nearest village, and she would follow us soon.

She came on her bicycle, seemed to have gotten over all her trouble, and looked very sweet and pretty. Then we all three went to Mrs. Tandie's house, I used to call it our coffee house, and, as always, spent a very cozy afternoon.

"What is grouse?" we asked Mr. Tandie when he told us that he would take a day off the coming week to be with some people who came each year for grouse shooting. "It's a kind of wild chicken, he said and promised after the shooting to bring some to the big house. Mr. and Mrs. Harrington were fond of them; he was hoping that we would like them too.

We heard the shooting, and I was afraid that my husband might refuse to eat one of these things, but he didn't make any remark and I didn't ask him either. Mr. Tandie kept his promise and brought four of these little birds and gave them to Mrs. Harrington. They were so small there was no fat on them and hardly any meat. To me they looked pitiful, and I wondered why one had to kill them in the first place. But Mrs. Harrington was delighted and told me they were considered a delicacy.

As I had no idea what to do with them, she told me to wrap strips of bacon around them and put them in the oven for roasting. While they were roasting, we prepared a sauce of bread crumbs and milk and a few slices of toast. The ready roasted grouse were then served on toast with bread crumb sauce on the side.

I didn't like them at all. They tasted bitter, and when I asked my husband how he like them, he said, "not particularly," but, as he was hungry, he was willing to eat anything as long as he didn't see it running or flying around.

My next visit to the dentist had to be postponed as we were notified to appear before the tribunal by the end of November. The tribunal was held in Glasgow, and we had to spend there most of the day. We waited around with the other refugees. All kinds of questions were asked, and all the answers were put down on paper.

At noon we were allowed to go out for lunch, but had to come back soon to answer more questions. We were afraid that if we had to wait much longer, we would miss our last train, but luckily enough we appeared before the judge just in time.

When all the answers were read, it was up to the judge which category he would assign us to. There were three categories:

A: meant interment camps for the duration of the war
B: meant five mile restriction
C: meant no restriction

We were very nervous, of course hoping for the Category C, and when the judge, after some considering, told us that he decided to classify us as C, I could have almost kissed him for joy. We thanked him and hurried out of the building, bought candies for Mrs. Tandie, and went to catch the train. We were so happy, we could hardly wait to tell everybody.

But first we wanted the Tandies to share our joy. They were our friends, our family, and everything we had in our new life. We went to their house before we went home and told them the good news. They were just as excited as we were. We had to tell them every detail, and they wouldn't let us go before we had a bite to eat.

Now we were to bring the news to Mrs. Harrington and hoped that she also would be glad for us. She was in the pantry, and, before she had a chance to ask how things went, we told that we were now classified as loyal and were now free to move around without a permit. She could see how we bubbled over with excitement, but her expression didn't change. She didn't say anything. This time she had an insignificant smile for us; no matter how disappointed we were, there was nothing we could do. It was a let down after a day that was so important to us, important not only because we didn't need a special permit when going further than five miles, but also because we thought the category C would make us what we really were, hostile to everything connected to Hitler and the countries whose purpose it was to cause war.

We realized that nothing would change the attitude of our employers, at least not for the time being, and so the days went by as before. Mrs. Peters went to the tribunal a few days later and was also assigned to category C.

We wrote to our friends and asked them how they had been classified, and to our great satisfaction we heard that they were also free to move around without a permit, and they were hoping to see us sometime in December.

Mr. Chamberlain's Reply to Hitler
Aggression Cannot Be the Basis of Peace

— *London Times,* October 13, 1939

British Troops In The Line
Artillery Takes Up Positions
Guns In Back-Gardens

— *London Times,* October 18, 1939

Women's Help In Evacuation
Nearly Half a Million Volunteers

— *London Times,* November 11, 1939

~ *10* ~

JUST AS late as spring and summer arrived in this part of the country, the winter was late in arriving. Autumn was still with us, and it was beautiful. We have never seen that display of colors; not only the leaves were changing from deep green slowly to gold and deep brown, but also the colors of the moors went even into purple; sometimes it didn't seem real. When the sun was out, the colors were bright, and before dawn there was a mist over the moors and it seemed like all the splendour would flow into one magnificent glow.

Strange as it was, we who when first arrived were almost depressed by the country side, now admired and even grew fond of it. The evenings were so peaceful; we often stopped at the Tandies', and after supper and going home, the castle and the grounds that surrounded it seemed enchanted.

The Hill family was still living in the cottage. We have not visited them yet and assumed that everything was running smoothly. But one morning Mrs. Tandie came over to the big house and soon Mrs. Harrington was in deep conversation with her. She was quite upset and told us too what it was all about.

The Hills were to move back again into their previous quarters, and, instead of telling us the reason in so many words, Mrs. Harrington told me to go along with Mrs. Tandie and see for myself. And there was quite a sight. The cottage looked just awful. The walls were dirty, the beds not made, and the coal range that Mrs. Tandie had polished with such care was full of spoiled food, and worst of all was the bathtub. Mrs. Hill either didn't believe in taking baths or didn't know what a bathtub was for; she put her coal in there instead. Or was it that it was too much trouble to carry the coal from the cellar? It was so much easier to have it handy near the range. And we had to admit with great regret that Mrs. Hill didn't learn anything as we all hoped she would. All those years she had to live in one room with her family could not be wiped out in the short time when she could live in comfort.

Mrs. Harrington was really afraid that the cottage would get neglected to such an extent that it could not be used in the future anymore. And that [was] why she decided to have the Hills move into the rooms which they occupied before, and she was resigned to put up with the smell hoping that it wouldn't last forever.

A few days after they moved back, one of the children got sick and ran a temperature, so Mrs. Harrington thought she better call the doctor. As long as the Hills lived in her house, Mrs. Harrington felt responsible for them and wanted them to have the right care.

I could never figure out why every time someone came to the house, Mrs. Harrington got all nervous and excited. Was it because so few people came, or had it something to do with India also? Anyway the doctor was supposed to come in the afternoon, and, in the morning, I already got orders to see that the kitchen was spotless, as the doctor had to come through the kitchen to the Hill quarters. She was so worried all day long that I was glad when the doctor finally arrived. He didn't even glance at the kitchen; all he wanted to see was the sick child.

After he examined it, he went into the morning room where Mrs. Harrington was waiting for him and gave her the result of the examination. While he was with Mrs. Harrington, he got thirsty and asked for a glass of water which my husband took in. Then he said he would be back in two days and left.

When he came back, the same procedure took place, only this time Mrs. Harrington instructed my husband to bring in a glass of water even though the doctor hadn't asked for it. But he wasn't thirsty and he didn't drink it; instead he looked at my husband holding the glass of water as if he wanted to ask if anything was wrong with him. After all he wasn't going to drink it if he didn't feel like it.

But Mrs. Harrington was not one to give up so easy. She told my husband that he should have served the water on a little silver plate, and then the doctor would not have refused it. When he returned two days later, the little silver plate didn't help either. He just wasn't thirsty.

Before he left, the doctor asked my husband to come out with him to the car. When my husband came back he had a little tablet in his palm and said that the doctor gave it to him just like that. He also told him something which he could not understand. We were both wondering what the tablet was for, and then I had an idea that the doctor wanted him to take it as he was the one who came closer to the Hill's room that any of us, and he wanted him to be on the safe side and not to catch whatever the child had. So he swallowed the tablet, felt a little funny afterwards, but was all right soon again.

In the evening the child's temperature went up, and, when Mrs. Harrington heard about it, she called the doctor again. She then came into the kitchen and asked what my husband did with the tablet the doctor gave him. So I told her that I told him to take it. She looked at me as if she had never seen me before and left the kitchen in a hurry.

I went on washing the evening dishes but couldn't get rid of the feeling that something was wrong. Why did Mrs. Harrington look at me that way, and why did she leave the kitchen as fast as she could? All of a sudden it came to me. Like a flash. The tablet and the child's fever; that tablet must have been for the sick child, and I told my husband to swallow it. Oh, did I feel like a fool.

But I had a reason why I assumed that the medicine was for my husband, and I left the dishes and now I went as fast as I could to explain it to Mrs. Harrington I thought I heard a chuckle in the morning room where both the Harringtons were, but they must have heard me coming because by the time I entered the room they had busied themselves with the crossword puzzle.

I came right out with my story. I told them that I had never seen a doctor give medicine into somebody's hand. Back home when we called a doctor, he gave us a prescription which we took to the apothecary. And I never would have thought that the tablet was for the child the way the doctor put it in my husband's palm without any wrapping or bottle; it just wasn't sanitary. "But around here in the country, there is no chemist (drug store) around," Mrs. Harrington said. "You are used to the city." That is true," I replied, "Though, still, he could have put it in a piece of paper or something." To myself, I thought that it wasn't even sanitary for my husband to take it that way, and certainly not for a third person.

The child's fever worried me too, but Mrs. Harrington said it was only a bad cold, and, should it get worse overnight, she would ask the doctor to come back. I was also glad that my husband had no aftereffect from swallowing whatever it was. All in all, I had a very bad time while the Harringtons, and probably the doctor too, must have had lots of fun. I remembered too when I told my husband when he made all these mistakes, that when I make one it would outshine all of his; I certainly kept my promise.

The child got well soon afterwards. The Hill family seemed to get ready to leave Yearkerscleugh. When we asked Mrs. Tandie why they were leaving, she told us that Mr. Hill, for some time now, wanted the family back home. He didn't feel like being alone, and he didn't think there was any danger for them to return to Glasgow. Mrs. Hill tried to delay their departure, but he insisted and finally declared that if she and the children wouldn't come home in a few days, he was going to get himself another woman.

Mrs. Hill could not, of course, take that risk; after all, he was the family provider. The oldest girl cried so hard when the time came to leave; she was old enough to realize what they had here and what awaited them in Glasgow. Poor kids. We grew so very fond of them just knowing they were around.

The little kitten stayed with us. We adopted her as our pet and called her "Pussy Cat." She followed us around, and, one day, Mrs. Harrington told me to go into Mr. Harrington's study and get her out of there because she would not listen to her. When I came into the study, she sat on Mr. Harrington's chair, looking so innocent as if she belonged there. But as soon as I called her, she followed me into the scullery where she had to be kept. We made a bed for her and saw that she had enough to eat, and she was so appreciative that she walked always around our legs.

One early morning, I thought that she would like some porridge, and I did what I never did before. I took out just a little from the porridge that the Harrington had every morning and which was left in the Aga Cooker over night, and was almost ready to put the saucepan back, when Mrs. Harrington appeared. She never came that early into the kitchen, and I didn't want her to know about the porridge because she didn't like the kitten. I felt quite embarrassed, like caught in the act, and I wondered what made her come just that day so early. It reminded me of the day she caught my husband sweeping the dust under the rug. She must have had a second sight.

Royal Visit to Girl Guides
National Service in War Time, The Queen's
Tribute

— *London Times,* November 14, 1939

"How to Win YOUR War of Nerves—Canatogen,
Nerve-Tonic Food"

— *London Times,* November 14, 1939

Knitting For The Forces
Heavy Demand For Wool and Needles

— *London Times,* November 21, 1939

"Home Recreation for the Black-Out"
Decca Records

— *London Times,* November 24, 1939

Round The Shops
Christmas Buying in Real Earnest, Ideas For
Practical Gifts

— *London Times,* November 27, 1939

~ *11* ~

BEFORE CHRISTMAS, there was a party in Aylesbury, and Mr. and Mrs. Engles, who lived in the other little cottage next to the Tandies, invited us to join them at the party. They took us and Mrs. Peters in their car to Aylesbury, where in a hall was quite a crowd of people singing, and, as soon as we arrived, Mr. Engels went to the piano and directed all the songs. He soon played, "We'll hang our washing on the Siegfried line." Everybody joined in, and we all sang at the top of our voices.

After the party, we all went to the Engles' house and had supper there. Mrs. Engles was an excellent cook and a wonderful housekeeper, and when I asked her where and when she acquired all her experience she told us that before she got married she also worked as a domestic servant. We talked about the different ways and habits of the different employers, and she mentioned that the servants were never to say "good morning" first. The lady or gentleman of the house or whoever was there was supposed to do it. A thought came to my mind how surprised Miss Ethel looked at me when I greeted her mornings. Well, I wasn't going to change it now. I have been saying "good morning" to the Harringtons before they had a chance to do it for so many months now they would just have to put up with it as long as we served them.

Once again the Harringtons had a little accident coming home from one of their outings. A pheasant ran out in front of their car and was killed instantly. They took it home, and Mr. Tandie cleaned it for us. He said he would bring another one, and Mrs. Harrington said they would have them for Christmas dinner. As there were two of them, Mrs. Harrington said we could have one for ourselves. The pheasants were to be prepared the same way as the grouse, but first they had to be kept a few days in the scullery so that the meat would get tender. Luckily again my husband didn't see the pheasant flying around, so I was pretty sure he would agree to eat them. This time Mrs. Harrington herself came down to the scullery to look the birds over and proclaimed them ready to be cooked. When I told her there were still two days before Christmas, she said, "We just have our Christmas dinner early; the birds are ready for the oven and have to be eaten. I don't want any flies around them again." The pheasant tasted so much better than the grouse, and we enjoyed the meal very much. To make the dinner more festive, Mrs. Harrington bought a special pie and gave us each a generous piece.

Since the Hills left, Mrs. Harrington was much more cheerful.

Her face didn't seem so tired anymore, and her smile was more re-laxed. She must have really suffered before.

I still had to have the last session with my dentist, and so we wrote to our friends about meeting them again. They let us know that they would have a few days vacation and intended to spend them in Glasgow. They wanted to know whether we could arrange to stay also for two or three days, but we didn't think we could. We were still to write and set a date as soon as we knew for sure what day we would be able to go.

Mr. and Mrs. Harrington made plans to go on a short holi-day to London. It was now the beginning of January, and we asked when we could have the day off, as I still had to see my dentist. She asked us to wait a few days, and, after they left, we could go too.

She was making all kinds of arrangements, and one thing she did upset us very much. When at any time before, they left for a day, nothing was changed around the house. We had access to all the rooms, and everything was left open. Now that they intended to leave for a few days, Mrs. Harrington had a lock made on the window ledge that led from the pantry to the dining room and through which the meals were served. We asked ourselves why in the world would she do a thing like that. Was she afraid that one of us would squeeze through the ledge and take something? But that wouldn't make sense; the doors would be left open, we thought. But they weren't. Before the Harrington left, every door was locked; only the back door and that that led to our rooms was left open. At first we were terribly hurt. If Mrs. Harrington would have just explained or used some kind of excuse why she took these kind of precautions, we would have felt better. But, as she didn't say a word, we could only assume that she didn't trust us. But why? We never gave her any reason to act the way she did now.

Or did she still resent us because of the war? Whatever it was made me really mad now. If she thought us not trustworthy then she should have let us go a long time ago. But to hurt us that way, that was not right. Well, if that was the way she wanted it, we didn't have to have responsibility for the house and we decided to have our revenge.

Under these circumstances we decided to take two or three

days vacation and spend them with our friends. We asked Mrs. Tandie to look after the pussy cat and Mr. Tandie 'promised to keep the Aga Cooker going. The we got in touch with our friends and arranged the rendezvous. The Harringtons were gone and we were hoping they wouldn't be back before us as we did not intend to tell them of our little escapade.

It was already afternoon when our friends arrived. As we were in Glasgow already in the morning, I had plenty of time to see my dentist and finally got my tooth. We went to the train to meet our friends and were then looking for a boarding house. After we secured the rooms, we went to have dinner and by the time we left the restaurant, it was dark. It was the first time that we saw a city entirely blacked out. Gerti and Oscar already experienced it as they lived in a small town. They carried each a torch (flashlight) and with its help we managed to find our way to the hotel.

For us it was an uncomfortable feeling to be walking in darkness, but all the other people seemed to have been used to it by now. They walked fast just holding their flashlights and holding them at a certain angle so that they wouldn't be seen from above. The whole city seemed to be full of lightning bugs.

Our rooms were so terribly cold, the coal fire was hardly there. We had to keep our coats on while sitting and talking until we went to bed. And even then I wished I had the bedsocks, Mrs. Tandie gave me for Christmas with me. That was a gift that I appreciated more than anything else, because also in Yearkerscleugh the beds were cold and after we undressed we had to dress for bed again.

Next morning, after a hearty breakfast, we went around the city exploring, buying a few things; the time went by only too fast. The boat from Ireland arrived the same afternoon and we all went to meet Oscar's brother. It was time for us to catch the train for Aylesbury, should we decide to go home already. As far as I was concerned, I would have stayed another day; I was very angry with Mrs.Harrington, but my husband didn't think we should overdo it. After all, we still had some responsibility toward our employers.

Once more we had to part and it was, every time, so difficult to say good bye. The Tandies were hoping that we will be back that evening because Mrs. Harrington arrived just a short while ago. It was not a pleasant situation; we didn't want that to happen, but now that it did, we had to face it. Mrs. Harrington did not say anything and didn't ask anything either, so I just said I had my tooth fixed and with that the matter was closed. Mr. Harrington arrived a few days later. The atmosphere has become tense to a certain extent and we were not sure anymore what to do. We considered leaving and one day made up our minds to go.

To find another job while we were still here was not easy but we wrote to a friend in London, inquiring about possibilities there. She answered almost immediately that she happened to know of a family who were looking for a couple; should we be willing to come to London we would, she was quite sure, get a job.

It was not easy to let Mrs. Harrington know about our decision. We were sentimental about the place and were sorry that things went the way they did. Well, maybe it was no one's fault; wars caused worse things than bad feelings.

And so it was I who told her that we would be leaving and gave four weeks notice so that Mrs. Harrington had plenty of time to find a replacement for us. She smiled, and I couldn't help but notice that her smile had an expression of relief. It was only for a fraction of a second there, but I was sure it was there.

She didn't seem to look for other help, and from Mrs. Tandie we heard that the Harringtons would be leaving Yearkerscleugh for the winter. We were quite surprised about that development, and had our own suspicion that they planned it for sometime, and, now that we were leaving too, it worked out fine.

A few days after we gave notice, we received a letter from a refugee committee in Glasgow. The letter said that the committee was notified by Mrs. Harrington that we intended to leave our job. The person who wrote the letter and who was in charge there wanted to know whether we were sure it was the right thing to do and if we had a place to go. We answered right away, gave the reason for our leaving, and told them that we had a good prospect for a job in London.

Mrs. Harrington puzzled us all over again. She could have asked us the same things that the committee asked; we would not have kept anything from her. Or didn't she want to discuss anything? We understood that she felt some responsibility towards us and wanted to part in the friendliest way possible as we would always be thankful for the permit we received when we needed it so badly.

We were supposed to leave early in February but had to postpone it as a snowstorm came to Yearkerscleugh. It was so bad, we were cut off from Aylesbury, and none of the merchants who delivered the groceries could reach us. Mr. Tandie and Mr. Engels put fishing boots on and worked their way to the village to get some food. In order to step out of doors, my husband had to build a tunnel through the snow, but first he had to reach through the upstairs window to shovel the snow away from the entrance door as it covered the whole height of the door. It looked as if the winter and the snow were going to stay for a long, long time. But we were in luck. The sun came out, and, after a few days, things began to get back to normal.

We left [in the] middle of February. We said good bye to Mr. and Mrs. Harrington the evening before. The worst part was to have to say good bye to Mrs. Peters. She would be so alone now; the only consolation was that we knew Mrs. Tandie would take care of her. And how sorry we were to part with Mrs. Tandie, our wonderful friend. She tried to make our [gap in original material]

It was not quite a year that we arrived in Yearkerscleugh, so alone and afraid of what was expected of us, and in that short amount of time we met such good and friendly people and learned to love the countryside.

We will always remember the sad and cheerful moments we spent here and the mistakes we made, and we would try to come back to see our friends. Right now we were on our way once again to more jobs, more experiences, and more people we knew nothing about. And when we saw Mr. Tandie standing there, waving until our car was out of sight, we knew that people like that would be hard to find.

And seven years later, exactly to the day we arrived in Britain, we left for the U.S.A. to be reunited with our family and to start a new life again in a country that was so different from the one we left behind.

SOME THOUGHTS ON CONTEXT AND MEANING;
OR, HOW TO READ AN OLD MEMOIR:
A COMMENTARY BY ERIKA BOURGUIGNON

> *Re-membered lives are moral documents and their function is
> salvific, inevitably implying, "all this has not been for nothing."*
> — *Barbara Myerhoff*

Why a Commentary?

Bronka tells a simple story, and she tells it simply. Yet as I read
it, and as I have told friends about it, I feel the need to place it
in context, historically, familially, culturally. How do the events
she tells of fit into the larger picture of the century and of the
particular period? What do we, fifty-some years later, know that
was perhaps not evident to those living the events and wondering
about the causes and the outcomes? To judge by the spate of recent
books, we are still wondering and arguing about the causes. Anne
Frank has had an "afterlife," and as Ian Buruma (1998) has shown,
how we read her story depends to some extent on who we are,
and when and where we are situated. How was it possible? And
just what did actually happen? The story of the Jewish accounts
in Swiss banks, which created excitement in 1997, is only one ex-
ample of the new information that causes us to reevaluate what
we thought we knew. Personally, I know that Switzerland gave us,
my parents and me, reluctant refuge for some fifteen months in
1938–39, while we waited for our American visas. And yet we were
threatened periodically with expulsion, and others were expelled.
Still others were never admitted. Some, later, were placed in labor

camps, and some did not survive. Hans Mayer, who spent the war years in such a Swiss labor camp, as a Jewish refugee from Nazi Germany, notes both the local anti-Semitism and the fear of anti-Semitism felt by Swiss Jews (1982–84). But he also notes how the defeat of France altered the situation and energized the anti-Nazi attitude of the Swiss under the leadeship of General Guisan.

How can we think about the past when we know so little about it, in spite of the large quantities of documentation? And when we work with oral history, how reliable is memory? (Langness and Frank 1981; Myerhoff 1978; Whiteman 1993; Wimmer 1990) Few people of Bronka's generation, of those who were not writers or intellectuals, wrote memoirs about the exile experience, and of those that were written fewer still were ever published. As members of the next generation — my generation — approach retirement, more of us seem to wish to look back, to talk about what happened, to seek out information, to bear witness while there is time, before the past is increasingly reworked into myth and stereotype, as has already happened to such a great extent. Here Bronka's document is important: It is now almost forty years old. It is written by a "naive" participant. Moreover, as a document dealing with a year in the lives of one refugee couple, it gives us more detail than do survey materials and interviews with a number of people. Being both subject and author, Bronka is free of the interviewer's questions and point of view. Most important, reading Bronka's memoir together with the broader literature we become acutely aware of the uniqueness of each person's story, in spite of the shared larger setting. It is this personal, individual uniqueness we must not lose sight of.

Looking back at the period that concerns us, I am struck by the ambiguity, the strangely contradictory and ambivalent character of so many of the actions and policies of the people the Jews looked to as potential saviors. In part this can be explained, on governmental levels, by the need to reconcile contending parties, the "political" nature of the decisions. This included the reluctance of both individuals and governments to believe reports of what was happening to the Jews in Germany and, later, in the territories occupied by the Germans. In the United States, it appears that there was in fact an official policy discouraging publication of information government agencies knew to be authentic. Britain made complex decisions to grant visas, generally thought to be temporary, to refugees from Nazism, while restricting Jewish immigration to Palestine in exercising its League of Nations Mandate. Complexity and duality also exist on the individual human level — for instance, there is the British housewife in need of servants, who may also be motivated by a desire to be helpful.

The following, then, is an attempt to provide context — or better, contexts — for Bronka's tale. We may start at the beginning, where Bronka begins, in Vienna.

Bronka's Vienna

Bronka begins her story with the Anschluss, the annexation of Austria by Germany on March 11, 1938, and with the period immediately following it. It may be helpful, however, to go a bit further into the past and take a brief look at Vienna and the Jews before these things happened.

Bronka says that "life in Vienna was good before Hitler came." Was it? Bronka was born in Cracow, in that part of the Austro-Hungarian monarchy called Galicia. It was a complex region, multilingual, with diverse religious and ethnic groups. The Jews who lived there — many in the sort of small market town known as (and now sentimentalized as) the "stetl," others in large cities — were not a homogeneous population. They were differentiated by class, religious adherence, occupation, language, traditionalism or "Enlightenment" (*Haskala*, which is not the same as assimilation), and political orientation. There were Hassidim and their opponents — Zionists (who favored Hebrew), and Socialists (who favored Yiddish). It was possible to be deeply rooted in Jewish culture and tradition and yet not be religiously observant.

Galicia is now divided between Poland and Ukraine. Bronka, like her siblings, attended a Polish-language primary school but also learned German. I don't think that much Yiddish was spoken in the home, although the children had Yiddish as well as Polish first names. Bronka's real name, after all, was Bronislawa, a classic Polish name; only her mother called her Blimtche. The family, with one son and three daughters, seems to have been comfortably middle class. I remember oil portraits of my grandmother's parents hanging in my grandparents' bedroom in their apartment in Vienna. There were large photographic portraits of another set of ancestors as well. When Bronka was eight years old, she also sat, or rather stood, for a portrait in oils. Other signs of middle-class status were a few small paintings, silverware, and jewelry, some of which have survived. I remember also the obligatory encyclopedia and sets of German classics in fine bindings. (Did anyone, besides me at age twelve or thirteen, ever read these?) Photographs of the trips to Bohemian spas that were customary in those days have survived, and there were other fragments of evidence of the family's social position, or aspirations.

Bronka's father, my grandfather, Lasarus (Leiser) Eichhorn, was, it seems, fearful of an approaching war and relocated his family to Vienna just before August 1914, when World War I did indeed break out. Bronka was fifteen years old.

Fin-de-siècle Vienna was a time and a place of great social, economic, and intellectual transformation, and the Jews of Vienna had an important role in all of this. Vienna was then one of the major cities of the world. With a population of more than a million, it ranked fourth in Europe, after London, Paris, and Berlin. Outside Europe, only New York was larger. In the 1980s Robert Waissenberger (who has been largely responsible for a series of publications on and discussions of the city and its remarkable achievements) organized an important traveling exhibition dedicated to turn-of-the-century Vienna. In a book associated with the exhibition, he writes that at the turn of the century "Vienna . . . experienced a brilliant efflorescence," but that, for a long time, its achievements "failed to gain adequate recognition" (Waissenberger 1984: 7–8). He suggests that this was because the artistic and intellectual developments were produced by and for the relatively small liberal bourgeoisie. There was a rapidly growing mass population, reflecting a dramatic expansion of industry; there were the tensions of a heterogenous society in an economically and politically archaic state. Jean Clair, introducing a catalogue of a parallel exhibition in Paris, takes a different view. He writes: "That Vienna, at the turn of the century, and more particularly between 1897 and 1907—the decade during which Mahler was the director of the Opera—was the geographic locus of an ensemble of political events, of ideological gambles, of artistic and literary creations of such importance that we are still today in their debt—no one would think to deny" (1986: 46; my trans.).

Waissenberger, who notes that no satisfactory explanation has been found for this turn-of-the century efflorence, concludes that the "role of the artist may be regarded to some degree as a prophetic one" (1984: 8) and suggests that creative production should be seen as a reaction to the "disquieting nature of reality" (7). Less poetically, one might argue that the cultural developments of Vienna of the late nineteenth and early twentieth century have to do precisely with economic changes that brought together large numbers of people with different social, cultural, and religious backgrounds and offered a market for their ideas and their products (Schorske 1980). The clash of cultures has always been productive of innovation, and the brilliant city attracted talent from outlying regions, in addition to the poor in search of work.

The stream of migrants that brought my grandparents to this rapidly changing city was only one of several. For example, by the turn of the century, 25 percent of the population of Vienna was made up of people from the Sudentenland. Largely of peasant origin, these people had come to work in the city's expanding industries (Düriegl 1984). As for the Jews, in 1910, when the population of Vienna had reached more than two million, they constituted 8.6 percent of the total. The first Jewish emigrants were from Bohemia and Moravia. Both Freud and Mahler belonged to this group. Later, increasingly, Jews came from Galicia, and also from Bukovina, the region to its south where Joseph was born.

Ethnic divisions among the Jews played a role in their social life. One of my mother's friends, a woman from Galicia, was married to a man from Moravia, then a part of Czekoslovakia. She maintained two circles of friends: "Ostjuden" and "Westjuden." Beyond ethnicity, there were class and occupation, political orientation, degree of religious adherence, and other divisive factors. Yet the Jews of Vienna were, on the whole, brought together into one offically recognized community, which represented them and to which they paid taxes: the *Jüdische Kultusgemeinde*. Also, Vienna never had the religious division between Conservative and Reform Jews which existed in Germany.

When the empire was broken up after the war, Bukovina became part of a larger Romania. Like Bronka's family, Joseph and his mother and sister also seem to have come to Vienna before 1914.

It may be helpful to remember that Jews have lived off and on in Vienna for close to a thousand years. In the summer of 1996, excavations for a memorial accidentally discovered the remains of a fifteenth-century synagogue in the *Judenplatz*, the heart of the medieval ghetto. However, Jews were also expelled periodically. The last time before 1938 was in 1670. Within a few years, they were gradually allowed to return, but at first only a small number of wealthy Jews was admitted. Much later, as a result of the French Revolution, with its Declaration of the Rights of Man, ghettoes were opened all over Europe and Jews were emancipated; the Austrian Empire, however, gave Jews full rights as citizens only with the constitution of 1867, barely seventy years before the events of 1938. Even with full citizenship, the work that Jews could do was limited, and they developed a distinctive occupational profile. According to one study (Oxaal 1990), in 1910 the Jewish population of Vienna was divided almost equally among the self-employed, employees in private firms, and workers in industry and commerce. Among non-Jews at the same time, three-quarters were industrial and commercial workers, less than 10 percent were employees, and only 14 percent were self-employed. Moreover, public employment was almost entirely closed to Jews, and this included the teaching profession at all levels, from grade schools to universities. One consequence of these restrictions was that Jews able to obtain a higher education (in spite of the *numerus clausus,* or admission quota) were concentrated in the so-called free professions: medicine, law, pharmacy, architecture, and so forth. Only a small percentage of Viennese Jews were wealthy, or famous as creative forces, whether as physicians or as intellectuals, writers, musicians, or artists. Throughout the period, the majority had trouble making ends meet.

Much has been written about the special character of Austria's endemic anti-Semitism. Mayer (1994) notes that at the end of the nineteenth century the Hapsburg monarchy was a complex, multinational state. In contrast to Germany, France, or Great Britain, which had relative ethnic and cultural homogeneity, the Austro-Hungarian monarchy might be called the original multicultural state. Within it, the German-speaking population was a minority. The enterpreneurial class (the "bourgeoisie") of the German-speaking area was a minority within that minority. The country's level of industrialization was low compared to neighboring Germany or the countries of western Europe, thanks to Metternich's policy, in the early years of the century, of keeping capitalism out and maintaining a largely agrarian society. As a result, the Austro-Hungarian monarchy was backward, what we would call today a "less developed" country. In this context, the German-speaking Jewish enterpreneurs were a minority within a minority (the bourgeoisie) within a minority (the German-speaking population). As industry developed, it was largely centered in and around the capital city of Vienna. Anti-Semitism, then, had roots in ethnicity, class, and religion.

To return to Waissenberger, there remains the interesting question of how the capital of such a backward, "archaic" country became the center of innovation in art, literature, and science, and how it is that people only recently emancipated could play such an important role in these developments.

World War I was a disaster for Austria. There were massive wartime losses almost immediately. The Russian armies moved into eastern Galicia (now Ukraine). My father, a law student, was in the first age class to be mobilized and soon was reported "missing in action, presumed dead." The family kept the document for many years. My grandmother, however, refused to believe her only son lost, consulted a so-called wonder-rabbi who gave her encouragement, and stoutly refused to go into mourning. She was vindicated: my father had been captured by the Russians, and he was able to escape to Sweden during the 1917 revolution.

With the severe fighting in Galicia, streams of refugees, including many Jews, began to arrive in Vienna soon after the war began. My mother was among them. During the war there were major food shortages, and people went hungry. Tuberculosis was rampant. On November 12th, 1918, one day after the Armistice, the emperor abdicated and the republic was declared. The postwar treaties, following Woodrow Wilson's demands for national self-determination, broke up the empire into a series of successor states cobbled together from disparate parts. The ethnic conflicts of Eastern Europe in the 1980s and 1990s bear witness to this history. Austria, the mostly German-speaking section of the old empire, now consisted of a very large capital city and a small mountainous hinterland: a city of 1.8 million in a country of 6.5 million. A third of the total population of Austria lived in the capital. There was a severe housing shortage, unemployment, and massive inflation. And quickly, various contesting groups appeared, some with strong voices calling for German-Austrian unification.

As the empire broke apart, Jews from war-devasted areas streamed into Vienna. Yet only those who, like Bronka and Joseph and my grandparents and parents, had arrived in time to make their claim were citizens of the new republic. Those who did not arrive in time, or did not understand the legal procedures or the cut-off dates, were not granted citizenship even though they might have had legal residence in Vienna. They were restricted from a variety of occupations, and many returned to the newly created independant Poland, which had been impoverished and devasted by the war.

By 1938 Jews constituted almost 10 percent of the population of Vienna, just under 200,000 people. In 1939, a year after the Anschluss, census figures reveal a radical reduction (82,077), but that number is inflated: it includes Jews defined as such by the Nuremberg race laws: persons with just one Jewish grandparent, regardless of whether they were baptized as Christians (Botz, Oxaal, Pollak 1990, p. 14). Gustav Mahler and Arnold Schoenberg might have belonged to that category, as might have sons or grandsons of converts, such as the writer Hugo von Hofmannsthal or the philosopher Ludwig Wittgenstein. Given the severely limited opportunities for Jews, conversion, in a very secular society, had often been seen as a practical matter. There were also a significant number of intermarriages.

After the war, then, times were hard. Once inflation had been brought under control, various attempts were made to reorganize. Vienna was an industrial city with a strong labor movement. The city government, under the control of the Social Democrats, created a vigorous system of city-sponsored housing, educational reforms, health insurance, school dental clinics, and other benefits. Domestic service was regulated, giving maids minimum wages and various protections. Even the word usage was changed: no longer maids in service (*Dienstmädchen*), they were now called household help (*Hausgehilfin*).

The national government, however, was dominated by the Catholic Social Party. Conflict between the parties, each of which had a private militia, threatened to tear the country apart. Twice, in 1927 and in 1934, armed conflict broke out between the workers and the state. These were not merely local events but signposts on the way to World War II. As Murray Sayle writes: "The supression of the Social Democratic Party's uprising against the newly established clerical-Fascist regime of Dr. Engelbert Dollfuss [in February 1934] was one of the pivotal events of the century, setting up sides for the Second World War" (1997: 14). He goes on to note that, "horrified to see the Austrian regular army shelling the workers' flats," various observers in Britain and the United States thought that "the Communists were offering the only effective resistance to Fascism." In 1929 the worldwide economic crisis, the Depression, hit, and it hit Austria hard. There was much unemployment and a great deal of hardship.

Bronka and Joseph had married in 1926. Both were employees in private enterprises. Joseph had studied at the Kunstgewerbeschule (School of Applied Art), specializing in fine cabinetry. This prestigious school, part of the city's artistic "efflorescence," had been established in 1868 in connection with the Museum of Art and Industry. It produced artists such as Gustav Klimt and Oskar Kokoschka (Schorske 1980). By the time he married Bronka, however, Joseph was an employee in the leather industry. I don't know how that happened, only that in middle-class Jewish families like that of my grandparents, working with one's hands was looked down upon. (So was higher education for women, but that is another story.) With the onset of the depression, Joseph almost immediately lost his job. He opened a small shop selling leather and supplies for shoemakers; shoes were then still largely made by hand in small workshops. Bronka was a bookkeeper for Phoenix, a large life insurance company. Its main offices were located in an eighteenth-century mansion in the elegant old center of the city, and I remember visiting her there. That company also failed, but not until 1936. Bronka, too, was then out of work, and she never held a job again in Austria. And though she writes, "Life was good before Hitler came," Joseph and Bronka did, in fact, experience rough times.

Then, too, there was the ever-present anti-Semitism, so constant that it seemed to be a fact of life. As Anton Walter Freud, one of Sigmund Freud's grandsons, has remarked, "Anti-Semitism was something natural, so that it wasn't necessary to talk about it" (Freud 1993: 21, my trans.). It meant that though Jews were not segregated residentially, in school, or on the job, they had little close social contact with non-Jews.

Vienna was a large city, however, and it offered many amenities, whether meeting friends in a café house, that essential Viennese institution, or hiking in the Vienna Woods and swimming in that branch of the Danube called *die alte Donau*. Bronka writes, too, of their part ownership of a small cabin and garden. This refers to a still-existing institution worth mentioning, the *Schrebergarten*. Based on the ideas of the physician by the name of

Schreber that urban life is unhealthy and that all families should have the opportunity to breathe fresh air (at least on the weekends) and to grow and eat fresh vegetables, several Schrebergarten were built on the margins of cities and found wide acceptance in both Germany and Austria. These were—and indeed, still are—small, tightly grouped plots with tiny cabins and minimal space for growing a few flowers and vegetables. Vienna also offered affordable cabarets, concerts, and theater performances, and, of course, family and friends. These are the things that made it a good life "before Hitler." But all that ended.

The anti-Semitism of the interwar period was not a new development. As noted earlier, anti-Semitism was a significant element in the lives of Austrians in the nineteenth century, in the period of the Monarchy, and, after the war, during the republic. Vienna's popular nineteenth-century mayor Karl Lueger used anti-Semitism skillfully for his political purposes. Hitler's own anti-Semitism seems to have taken shape during his unsuccessful stay in Vienna (Schorske 1980). In times of economic difficulties, anti-Semitism turned Jews into scapegoats; the Catholic Church, and its political arm, the Christian Social Party, who controlled the government between the time of the workers' uprising in February 1934 and the end of the Austrian republic in March 1938, exploited anti-Jewish feelings in its conflict with the Social Democratic Party, many of whose leaders were Jews. For the Nazi Party, of course illegal in Austria—from the time of the assassination of Chancellor Dollfuss by Nazis in 1934—it was a major rallying cry.

The Anschluss *and the* Märztage: *The "Days of March"*

By March 1938, when Germany invaded and annexed Austria, Hitler and the Nazis had been in power in Germany for five years, during which time anti-Semitic laws and regulations had been introduced gradually and cumulatively. The full set of practices that had developed in Germany over the years was brought to Austria in one piece. In addition, there was in Austria a series of more or less spontaneous outrages directed against Jews of a type that had not ever been seen in Germany. These were the days of March, the Märztage.

Bronka describes the anxiety and slender hope she, her husband, their friends, and their relatives experienced during this period. A number of topics are mentioned regularly in reports of the first weeks after the Anschluss, and Bronka's account is consistent with them. The indignity of forcing Jews to scrub the streets on their hands and knees, initally to clean off anti-annexation slogans for a plebiscite that never happened, is perhaps the most frequently noted. This particular humiliation has been recorded in often reprinted photographs of the word press, and has been memorialized in a monument placed near the Vienna Opera House. More than fifty years after these events, Arthur Miller made a newspaper picture showing old men scrubbing streets a key theme in his play *Broken Glass* (Miller 1994). Of course, the victims were not only Jews with beards and earlocks, wearing black caftans. Any "Jewish-looking" person might be picked up, that is, any one with supposedly "Jewish" features who was not wearing the Nazi swastika. Sometimes there were mistakes: apparently, a Nazi propagandist was beaten up (this episode was turned into a song), and some staff members of the Italian embassy were arrested. Doris Liffman, a medical student at the time, describes being accosted by a young man with the question "Miss, are you Jewish?" and then being asked to follow him and wash windows. After half an hour she was sent home (Gaisbauer 1996: 60). Another young physician found herself dismissed from the medical society for being a Jew but then received a letter releasing her, as a physician, from such street cleaning (Mahler-Schachter 1993).

As Saul Friedländer has noted, "The persecution of the Jews in Austria, particuarly in Vienna, outpaced that in the Reich. Public humiliation was more blatant and sadistic; forced emigration more rapid. The Austrians . . . seemed more avid for anti-Jewish action than the citizens of what now became the Old Reich [*Altreich*]" (1997: 241). And Gerhard Botz quotes an article in the Vienna edition of the official Nazi paper, the *Völkische Beobachter,* of April 26, 1938, warning the local populace that "the Nazis professed a commitment to responsible education of the public . . . to stem the exuberant local antisemitic radicalism, steering the understandably violent reactions to the Jewish excesses of a whole century into orderly channels. This means, and let everyone take note, because Germany is a state based on the law: nothing happens in our state except by due process of law. . . . There will be no pogroms, certainly not through Mrs. Hinterhuber wanting to get at Sarah Cohen, in the third courtyard, on the half-landing, by the watertap" (1987: 187). This is a remarkable document. The (German) Nazi Party as well as the government — if such a distinction is possible — looked with distaste at the apparently spontaneous violence and unbecoming lack of discipline of the Viennese. They were aware of international press coverage and foreign (and perhaps even domestic) public opinion. Walter speaks of these weeks as "pandemonium" directed against Jews and of "the hounding of Jews as popular celebration" (1992: 346). The German text reads: "Judenhatz als Volksfest." According to the dictionary, *Hatz* means "hunt, coursing; pack of hounds; rout, tumultuous revelry." In Vienna, the dialect form of that noun, *eine Hetz,* means "fun," a "ball."

Jewish men were routinely arrested on the street or at home to be sent off to concentration camps such as Dachau and Mauthausen. These were not yet extermination camps, although people died there and their families were told they had been "shot, attempting to flee." The primary purpose of these arrests seems to have been to terrorize the Jewish population. Men were released, often with payment of extorted sums of money, and then expelled from the country. Individual policemen had to meet a daily or weekly quota of arrests. Sometimes there were denunciations, and people were arrested in their apartments and the apartments themselves confiscated. That happened to our downstairs neighbors, and the apartment was turned into Nazi Party offices. The concierge thought it was too bad, "such nice people." But she also thought that there were others to whom it should have happened. Our new "neighbors" made my father's daily habit of listening to BBC broadcasts a bit more anxiety producing.

The harrassment and persecution began immediately after the arrival of the German troops. After about six weeks, that is, by the end of April 1938, the government called a halt to the popular "exuberance" and moved on to so-called legal means to harass and exclude the Jews. But it was not all a matter of appearances and public relations. As Botz writes, "Berlin had expressed concern that 'in Austria there had occurred widespread confiscation of property' which had been impossible to control. Therefore, measures were taken to reign in the pogrom. This led to a phase of seemingly legal actions whose function it was to prepare the further progress of anti-Jewish measures" (1987: 189). Bronka mentions items in the repertory of harassment that have been cited less often in reports of the period, but that speak clearly to the atmosphere of anxiety. One I, too, remember well was the fear of being separated and interrogated by plainclothes policemen in the street and the resulting need to agree beforehand on a topic of conversation when walking with another person.

In the summer of 1938, shortly after my parents and I were able to leave Austria, an edict required Jews to add either Sarah or Israel to their names. When our passports had to be renewed during our stay in Switzerland, Sarah became my middle name by authority of the German consulate in Geneva, although my parents, living in Zurich, did not have this change imposed on them by the consul there. More important, our passports were marked with a red "J" for Jude. (We now know, as we did not then, that this was actually done at the request of one Heinrich Rothmund, then head of the Swiss Federal Police, to help him keep track of Jewish refugees.) In Austria (and the rest of Germany) all Jews from the age of fifteen were then required to carry a special identity card. The harassment intensified month by month, week by week, indeed, day by day.

For example, in April 1938 the number of Jewish university students was reduced; a few months later, Jews were fully excluded. Jewish secondary students were expelled and driven to a small number of special Jewish schools. Expulsions from primary and trade schools followed quickly. Jewish teachers were dismissed. By the end of the 1938–39 school year, all public education and most private education for Jewish children was eliminated. In a moving autobiography, Elizabeth Trahan describes her life as a Jewish teenager in Vienna during the war years (1997a, 1997b). As they did not have children, Bronka and Joseph were not directly affected by the decrees involving schooling, but the decrees affected their friends and contributed to the general atmosphere of fear.

Increasingly, Jews were eliminated from the professions and limits were placed on their employment and business ownership. At the same time there was governmental concern not to harm the economy too greatly by affecting general production and commerce, including export. After all, Jews still made up almost 10 percent of the productive and gainfully employed population. There was also the matter of the spontaneous takeover of Jewish businesses. Botz quotes Reich-Commisionary Bürckel expressing concern over the "extent of robbery and theft" in Austria in the first few weeks, which caused him to take action and set up rules (Botz 1987: 192). For Jews, so-called aryanization meant expropriation. Friedländer notes that by August 1939, that is, seventeen months after the German occupation, all of the 33,000 Jewish-owned business enterprises of pre-Anschluss Austria had been "aryanized" or liquidated (1997: 243). In present-day Vienna, there are still businesses, department stores, and specialty stores that carry the names of their pre-1938 Jewish owners. Bronka writes, "We had lost all ability to make a living." Indeed, I recall that while we were living in Switzerland between the summer of 1938 and September of 1939 (when we were finally able to leave for the United States), Bronka and Joseph mailed their books to my parents, a few at a time, to be sold for whatever price that could be gotten.

Emigration

The German government made its intentions quite clear: Austria (like the rest of Germany) was to become "*judenrein*" — cleansed of Jews. The major means of bringing this about was to provide every "encouragement" for Jews to emigrate. By the summer of 1938, monies confiscated from wealthy Jews were used to expedite the emigration of poor Jews. Yet at the same time, a series of obstacles were set up to hinder emigration. A desire to leave clearly was not enough; a destination was also needed, a country that would accept the would-be immigrants. And once in a new country, the arrivals would need to find ways of making a living. Bronka tells us something of relevance about each facet of this complex and fearful situation. And here, too, her account is consistent with that of others (e.g., Whiteman, 1993).

Bronka describes well the various efforts of Jews, hoping for passage out of Austria to improve their skills and prepare themselves for new lives under unknown circumstances. Various informal instructional venues sprang up. Women sought to become better cooks and bakers, or to improve their infant and childcare abilities or their artisanal skills. Some of these training efforts were initiated by volunteer organizations, some by the Jewish community. In addition to working on her cooking, Bronka, I recall, also learned to cut and sew leather gloves and to string pearls. It is noteworthy in this regard that it was women's traditional skills that were thought to provide a more reliable basis for employment. Bronka had been an accountant with a major firm, yet she seemed, rightly, to have had little hope that such professional skills might be transferable to another country.

Retrospectively, we can see that it was indeed true that traditional women's skills in childcare, cooking, and homemaking had significant survival value for migrants. And this is still true in the 1990s, when Caribbean, Latin American, and East European women find such employment in the United States, even though they might have been teachers, architects, or middle-class housewives in their own countries.

Men had—and have—no obvious "natural" skills and often found their reduction in job status or their inability to find suitable work demeaning and humiliating. This idea of women's "natural" skills and, as a result, their greater adaptabilty must be viewed with some caution, however. On the basis of a series of oral history interviews, Marion Berghahn concludes that most German-Jewish women refugees in England had come from well-to-do homes and "had first to acquire basic housework skills such as cooking" (1984: 292). As a result, they experienced "a particularly radical readjustment." On the whole, it is likely that, before 1938, the well-to-do were better able to find ways of escaping from Nazi Germany than the poor were. On the other hand, the integration of many well-to-do Jews may have rendered them both less willing to recognize the dangers that confronted them and more afraid to start a new life under unfamiliar and difficult conditions. German laws made it impossible to take significant assets of any kind out of Nazi-occupied territory, and diplomas were, for the most part, not honored accross borders.

The necessary occupational changes were initially viewed as a means of survival. Once in a new country, the hardships could best be borne by thinking of the dangers from which one had just escaped. Hardship was seen as a temporary necessity and hope was tendered for a better future ahead. During the war, this situation seemed to be only "for the duration," as the phrase went in the United States. Beyond that, the future was unknown, but surely it could only be better! As such, it became the subject of much fantasy — a fantasy that did not always turn into reality. And this often had psychological as well as practical consequences.

Emigration required visas, admission to another country, payment of different taxes, various exit papers, and passports. The United States required an affidavit of support from a sponsor and a health check; tuberculosis and trachoma were high on the list of diseases warranting exclusion. More critically for a larger number of would-be refugees, the United States had quotas for immigrants. These quotas, enacted in 1924 and based on Census figures of 1890, were allocated by country of birth, not of citizenship. And "country of birth" referred to the post-Versailles borders of Central and Eastern Europe. Under these rules, Bronka was assigned to the Polish quota and Joseph to the Romanian. The Polish quota had a long waiting period; the Romanian was worse. And so, though they registered with the American consulate, they needed to find some other place of refuge in the meantime.

Great Britain had several categories of visas: There were some for scholars and artists, invited by universities and institutes. Children were admitted based on exceptional circumstances; they came to Britain to live with foster families or to stay in special homes organized by Jewish charitable agencies. Since this was seen as a temporary expedient, siblings were often separated, with the expectation that they would later be reunited with their parents. In many cases, of course, this did not happen. A total of ten thousand children came to Britain in these *Kindertransporte*. In recent years a number of survivors have published their accounts (e.g., Greshon 1966). Berghahn calls the *Kindertransporte* an "unparalelled achievement which probably saved the lives of no less than 10,000 emigrants" (1984: 290). Yet, as in many of the elements that make up the complex history of the period, there is another aspect to this story. In a 1997 book about Ben-Gurion and the Holocaust, Shabtai Teveth pointed out that Britain's decision to admit 10,000 Jewish children shortly after the Kristallnacht was linked to its refusal to grant visas for Palestine to these children. This linkage has had an afterlife in Israeli politics.

Another British visa category was that of domestic service. Little has been written about this, whether from the perspective of the refugee domestics themselves or that of their employers. Only after many years had elapsed did scholars such as Berghahn (1984, 1988) and Kushner (1991) turn to both documentary sources and oral history interviews to investigate the subject. Kushner has entitled one study of refugee domestics "Asylum or Servitude?" thereby expressing the ambiguous, ambivalent nature of the enterprise (1988). For some, it was surely both. About twenty thousand refugees came to Britain as domestics, originally as part of a scheme to solve the middle class servant problem and only later as in part a humanitarian gesture designed to save people.

Surprisingly little research has been done on the experience of domestics in general, and on British domestics in particular. Even with the development of the field of women's studies, little is known about an area where the employment and working conditions of women are situated within the household and are generally controlled by a woman. What has been published for the most part deals with Latin America and the U.S. (e.g., Nett 1966, Gill 1994, Rollins 1985, Sanjek and Cohen, eds. 1990), which is not directly relevant to the situation that concerns us. One exception is the work of Pam Taylor, who studied domestic service in Britain between the wars (1980). She does not mention foreign servants but states that there was a significant increase in the number of domestic servants in the years 1921–31 (16 percent) and that in 1931 almost a quarter of British working women were in domestic service. There was a desperate need for work among working-class women, particularly in areas of high unemployment, and girls as young as fourteen were sent off to work as domestics at the end of their obligatory schooling. In this context, middle-class, middle-aged foreign adults clearly represented a different category of servants, one whose behavior must have often puzzled their employers. For both servants and employers, the key issues appear to be class differences and differing expectations based on varying cultures and traditions. The experiences Bronka describes give us occasion to return to this point.

In spite of the depression, there was a servant shortage in England during the interwar period, a time when the demand for servants actually expanded. Although there was opposition from unionized British domestics, servants were recruited from other countries, specifically Germany and Austria, whose economies had been devastated by World War I. Of the Jewish refugee women from Germany and Austria who came to England after 1933, over half originally came as domestics. As Kushner notes in a rare major study: "Even in domestic service the refugees, often seen as totally unsuitable for their new occupation, actually brought improvements and innovations in cooking and home care to the technologically backward and conservative British household" (1991: 555). Kushner also says that treatment of servants ranged from sympathetic, helpful households to those who, in the words of a Ministry of Labour official, "regarded domestic servants as an inferior race and treated them accordingly" (1991: 566). As we see in Bronka's reports not only of their own experience but also of that of their friends and acquaintances, there was indeed considerable variation in attitudes and behavior of employers and, indeed, also of the domestics themselves. It is tempting to speculate that some basis for the different attitudes of employers lay in their own class position and the tradition of treating servants in which these women were schooled.

In Germany and Austria, in response to the perceived opportunity in Britain, various training programs for domestics were developed by Jewish agencies, specifically the Jüdische Frauenbund, the Jewish Women's Association. Some schools to train men as butlers were also created.

Beginning in the 1930s, the British government began to control the conditions of domestic employment and also to structure specific immigration policies. According to Kushner, in 1939, the year that interests us specifically in this story, "a limited number of domestic permits for married couples were introduced" (1991: 562). At that time, a prearranged post was also required, as well as a commitment to the job for a fixed period of time. And that is how it came about that Bronka and Joseph went to Britain as a couple.

While Bronka and Joseph prepared for emigration and waited desperately for the opportunity to leave, the Nazi regime continuously intensified its restrictions on Jews. Then came the infamous *Reichskristallnacht* and the following day, November 10, 1938. Bronka's muted description is touching. Joseph puts on his coat and waits to be picked up. There is no place to flee or to hide. Clearly orchestrated from above, the pogrom is called off at 5 o'clock. Now departure became ever more urgent, yet it took several more months before it became a reality for Joseph and Bronka — under the circumstances, almost a miracle. That the process was perhaps hastened by a letter from my father in Switzerland to the agency in Scotland was something I did not know until I read this memoir. Only in March of 1939 were Bronka and Joseph able to leave, a full year after the Anschluss. During that time, the persecution of Jews had intensified, and the march toward war in Europe had steadily advanced.

Domestic Service in Scotland

Bronka begins her tale with a letter she received (but from whom?) telling her of the destruction by fire of "Yearkerscleugh," the castle in Scotland where she and her husband had spent their year as domestic servants. The year was 1960, and they were then living in Peoria, Illinois, the proverbial American small town. It is this letter, she says, that set her to reminiscing. And it is this opening that makes me wonder whether she had read Daphne Du Maurier's *Rebecca.* That story, too, begins with the narrator's memory of a country house destroyed by fire. For me, Bronka's opening conjures up movie images of British country houses, houses, like this one, set in great parks in the countryside, far from the nearest village or town. Like such fictional places, the castle of Yearkerscleugh is a building comprising different sections, added to here and there, with the oldest part dating back to the sixteenth century. But when Bronka and Joseph arrive, they have only the vaguest idea of where they are, what the house is like, what kind of people with whom they will be living, and upon whom they will be depending.

As it turns out, they are in a castle set in the moors, somewhere in southern Scotland. In Austria, too, Bronka tells us, there were castles, but they were mostly in ruins and known mainly as tourist sites. (She could not have imagined that in the 1990s Austrian castles might be turned into American-run bed and breakfast tourist accommodations.) Here, however, was an ancient family seat, recently reacquired by a descendant. The house was, she suggests, located at roughly equal distance from Glasgow and Edinburgh, and at two hours' walking distance from the nearest railroad station in the village she calls Arlington. There are few people in the area, but lots of sheep.

There are a great many adjustements to be made. Indeed, almost everything is strange to the new arrivals. Bronka understood and spoke some English; Joseph, it appears, much less, and some of both the humor and the pathos of the tale hinges on misunderstandings and mistakes due to language difficulties, particularly Joseph's. Although Bronka presents him as somewhat bumbling, she also shows him as being more reflective and serious-minded than she. While Mrs. Harrington, their employer, speaks, it seems, standard British English, the gardner and his wife, Mr. and Mrs. Tandie, are much more difficult to understand. But in both cases there are many unfamiliar turns of phrase and many other topics. These range from details of etiquette regarding handshaking to food and domestic arrangements. That servants are not to initiate conversations with employers, even to say a polite "good morning," is something Bronka finds out only very late in the story. How could one guess such a rule?

Among refugees from Austria, it was often said that those who found the means to stay in Europe were the lucky ones. That, of course, was before the war broke out and so much of Europe overrun by the German armies or, like Britain, endangered. The point was that Europe, somehow, was home, and that any form of European life, however great the difference, was still more familiar than what might be expected in such faraway places as America — often imagined as the Wild West, as Sinclair Lewis's *Main Street,* or New York's Lower East Side of Michael Gold's autobiography, *Jews without Money.* Many were familiar with these books, which had wide readerships in German translation. Australia, Africa, Latin America, or China, where some landed, were beyond imagination. (In 1997 an exhibition was held at the Ethnologische Museum of St. Augustin (in Germany) entitled "Juden in China." It dealt not only with the early settlement of Jews in Kaifeng — discovered there by Matteo Ricci in the 1500s — but also with the nineteenth- and twentieth-century settlement in Shanghai — even during the Japanese occupation (see also Kranzler 1976). (The father of our cousin Hans Hirsch, who himself went to England in a Kindertransport, ended up in Shanghai, having missed the expiration date of the visa allowing him to go to England as a butler.) It is important to remember that, in spite of the underlying constants in the stories of this period of Jewish emigration and exile, really no two stories are quite the same.

Bronka gives us the opportunity to consider the minutiae of life in Yearkerscleugh and to watch the protagonists of this tale find something strange and often incomprehensible at every point of their daily lives. To begin with, there is the house and its setting: the people, the furnishings, the food, the daily routine. There are also the moors themselves, a landscape unlike any Bronka and Joseph had ever known, which contributes to their sense of displacement. While they are received politely and kindly by their employer, Mrs. Harrington, used to English and Indian servants, seems to feel no need to give these strangers any kind of information about where they are and only little about what will be expected of them. Matters are revealed only gradually, and Bronka makes that part of the mystery she unfolds before us. Who are the people? What are the tasks to be carried out and the objects to be handled, starting with the heavy woolen blankets on the beds, the fireplaces, and the kitchen stove? And the foods to be prepared. For Joseph, there is food to be served at the table and cleaning chores—and this for a man unlikely to have ever done housework of any kind, although he had prepared himself with butler training before emigrating.

The striking thing is how many of these items, which might be read simply as an inventory of life in a British country house some sixty years ago, turn out to involve cultural contrasts. As Central Europeans, Bronka and Joseph were used to down comforters, not tucked-in woolen blankets. They were familiar with tile stoves, not open fireplaces. Cooking was done with gas, not coal or oil. Urban life involved connection to an electric grid, not self-sufficiency, with a generator to be cranked up daily. Food was purchased daily in stores—there was neither the weekly delivery nor the kitchen garden and the surrounding farms. And then there is the matter of wildlife. In rural Scotland, where wildlife abounds, hunting is a tradition, and eating roadkill is sensible practice. Central European Jews had no tradition of hunting, and game animals were not perceived as edible—at least in part because they were not kosher. And so it is not only Joseph's attachment to the "charming rabbits" he sees on the road that makes the story of his resistance to rabbit stew understandable; the tale also shows how the dependent status of the servant makes for the development of deviousness, in this instance to avoid giving offense. This might be a good place to mention that while Bronka had kept a kosher house in Vienna, mostly out of respect for her mother, preparing and eating non-kosher food in Britain seems not to have been an issue for her. It is also striking that the topic of religion never comes up. None of the actors in this tale seem to engage in religious practices; no minister or rabbi is mentioned. The word *religion* appears only in connection with Nazi persecution of Jews.

The story of the tiger skin illustrates another aspect of the "alienness" of life in this Scottish castle. It also demonstrates the incomprehension of these urban, Central European Jews of the pleasures of the hunt, and it illustrates the failure of an attempted gesture of kindness or generosity.

In her autobiographical novel *Other People's Houses,* Lore Segal describes a telling scene of interaction between mistress and servants. The narrator's parents, Austrian Jewish refugees, are employed as cook and gardener by an English family. In true *Upstairs, Downstairs* fashion, the woman is addressed as Mrs. but the gardener only by his last name. The wife asks the lady of the house whether he might not be addressed as Mr. The employer finds that unacceptable—gardeners are never called Mr. This middle-class man finds himself degraded by this loss of respect. Bronka notes her own astonishment when she is first addressed by first name and Joseph only by last name. The loss of titles of address and respect came as a shock, a confirmation of their change in status. Yet, at least retrospectively, she says they were able to take it in stride, and she reflects on it with some amusement. I recall Joseph, famous for his humor, saying in a letter to my parents in Zurich that his job at the castle was to be the ghost.

Specialized professional skills and the sense of achievement and identity linked to them lost their value to a significant extent, and migrants were, and felt, declassed. Many never recovered their earlier sense of self worth, and for people with children, that recovery of status was often a goal passed on to the young. In the United States, after all, that is the standard immigrant story. Britain, however, did not have a tradition of immigration and social mobility.

Bronka describes how she told her new friend Mrs. Tandie about their life in pre-Hitler Vienna. Given the picture she paints of the Tandies' rather isolated life in rural Scotland, a life Bronka finds so foreign, one might wonder how strange or incomprehensible Mrs. Tandie might have found Bronka's accounts. What might have been her picture of a Viennese café, a Schrebergarten, the Vienna Woods, or the Alte Donau? What Bronka herself seems to have remembered vividly are the differences she notes. And, as in the case of "early tea," this leads to reflections, discussions with Joseph, and comparisons. What we have here, then, is an example of the alien, the exile, as ethnographer!

Once war broke out in September 1939, things changed, in a number of ways. The refugees were placed under surveillance, cameras were confiscated, and any trip beyond a five mile radius now required special permission. Their employers became both anxious and somewhat suspicious, though in their undemonstrative way, they said nothing. Yet by their actions, it becomes increasingly clear that trust has somehow been reduced. Throughout the country, thousands of refugee domestics were dismissed and some were interned. For the refugees themselves, including Bronka and Joseph, the war also meant they they were now cut off from relatives and friends still on the continent. There was now no news and no means of providing any help to them.

The war intrudes into this quiet life not only with the very presence of the Central European refugees but also with the arrival of evacuees, a Glasgow slum family. Bronka feels sorry for the children and shows surprising understanding for the woman, in addition to horror at her slovenly life. Bronka attributes her disastrous housekeeping to a lack of learning. The story shows both Mrs. Harrington's civic-mindedness in accepting these people into her home and also her unwillingness to confront the woman. Just as later she will not confront Bronka and Joseph about their unauthorized absence or about their reasons for leaving, here, too, she operates by indirection. Again, the difference in behavior be-

tween the formal English Harringtons and the friendly Scots, the
Tandies, is evident. Mrs. Tandie is full of warm concern for Bronka
and Joseph and seems to understand how the war makes their
separation from their kin so much more threatening.

Among these strangers in a remote rural area, Bronka and
Joseph feel alone and isolated as well as frustrated and bored by
the monotony of their lives. Even early in their Scottish year, when
they are able to meet Viennese friends in Glasgow on their day off,
there is great pleasure in talk. Indeed, Bronka refers to the impor-
tance of talk and the sharing of experiences repeatedly throught
the memoir. Here, I suggest, we may find a reason for her under-
taking the writing of these reminiscences so many years later.
Bored and isolated in Peoria, writing for her may well have been a
(temporary) substitute for talk, a way of sharing with others things
that had happened, of retelling the story of a significant part of
her life. Regarding the Glasgow visit, she comments perceptively,
"Everything that used to be so easy back home and was taken for
granted like meeting our friends took on such a different and im-
portant meaning now." In Glasgow, too, there is pleasure in being
waited on in a restaurant, in having her hair done, to receive rather
than to give services.

Looking back at these accounts from the perspective of the
1990s, the rural Scotland of 1939 seems remarkably isolated. It is
difficult for us now to imagine a world without the constant con-
nections of television and rapid travel. So little world news made
its way to Bronka and Joseph that it was difficult for them to
keep up with developments. On the other hand, as average Central
European middle-class people, they know little of Britain and vir-
tually nothing of Scotland. Scottish history and nationalism, what
they learn of it, comes as a total surprise.

There was then a Jewish community in Scotland, and there
were refugee organizations and Jewish volunteer support organi-
zations (Kölmel 1984). Bronka and Joseph seem not to have en-
countered any of them or to have sought them out. Here, as in
their later life, they seem to remain in transition, moving through
countries, regions, and languages. Interestingly, their English em-

ployers, the Harringtons, also seem to be "displaced" people, returning before the start of the war, after many years in India, to a drastically changed Britain and installing themselves in a recently acquired house. Mrs. Harrington's fear of flies seems unreasonable in the Scottish context, as does her rejection of canned meats. She has to deal with foreign servants, a cook who prepares strange foods, blackouts, and evacuees with destructive housekeeping habits — even the proverbial coal in the bathtub of the poor. And a husband whose tastes in food she misjudges.

Epilogue

Bronka concludes her story with a "happy end" — being released from service by a kindly judge at the end of a year, and then, in the spring of 1946 after seven years in Britain, being able to join her family in the United States. Matters were not as simple as all that, however. After the invasion of Holland and Belgium, the evacuation of British forces from Dunkirk in May 1940, and the capitulation of France in June, Britain was alone in the war against Germany. There was great anxiety and suspicion of all foreigners. Because they held German passports or were stateless persons, refugees from Nazi Germany were defined as "enemy aliens" in Britain, as they were, after December 7, 1941, in the United States. German nationals were interned, as were some others. Internment applied mostly, but not entirely, to men. Joseph was interned on the Isle of Man, in the Irish Sea. The British did not differentiate among German aliens, and Jewish and political refugees were often grouped with Nazis. Joseph was then forty-seven years old. Younger men were shipped to Canada or Australia, some came back to serve in the (unarmed) Pioneer Corps, and some, eventually, in the British Army. In a 1996 film, Wendy Oberlander tells of her father's wartime experience in such a Canadian internment camp. In the United States, once the country entered into the war in December 1941, "enemy alien" status, even for people who had their "first papers" (the initial step toward citizenship) resulted in fingerprinting and a prohibition against owning shortwave radio receivers. (In his 1984 autobiography Jimmy Ernst tells the bizarre story of the encounter between his father, the German surrealist painter Max Ernst, and the FBI because of his shortwave radio and how he was "saved" by Peggy Guggenheim.)

When the Blitz, the period of intensive bombing of London, began, Bronka, like many others, moved north, first to Nottingham, then to Oxford, where she stayed for the duration of the war. There she worked as a salesclerk. There were other refugees in Oxford who had come from London, including my mother's oldest sister, who had also come to England as a servant. Bronka was helpful and attentive to her.

We don't know exactly when Joseph was released from internment. It certainly lasted several months, and he had stories to tell about his various companions in misfortune. The camp experience has been discussed by various writers (Kochan 1983; Seyfert 1984; Davidson 1991; Furst 1994; Gillman and Gillman 1980, and numerous others). The island was safe from German bombardment, it seems, and, according to some, food was plentiful. Moreover, the camps "were centers of great cultural and educational activity" organized by the internees (Davidson 1991: 542). Still, internees were deprived of their freedom, separated from their families, and faced an uncertain future.

For a time after his release and after the war, then, Joseph worked in the textile industry, in a job that involved matching of patterns, tasks that called on his craft training and visual skills. His first love remained working with wood. In this he influenced a young cousin, to whom he left his tools.

In speaking of the time "before Hitler," when "life was good," Bronka calls Austria "our country." In the 1960s, when Joseph retired, Bronka and Joseph were able to take a trip to England and enjoyed visiting friends and relatives. They also went to Israel, again visiting friends and relatives, staying in a boarding house, as I recall, run by a woman from Vienna and feeling quite at home. But no trip to Austria was undertaken or contemplated; that part of their lives had been cut off and could not be recuperated. It must be said here that the Austrian government of the postwar years made no overtures to those it had forced to flee and for almost fifty years made no acknowledgement of its role in the persecution of Jews. In 1943 the Allies declared Austria "the first victim of Hitler's aggression." The active and enthusiastic collaboration of a substantial portion of the Austrian population was not acknowledged. As Egon Schwarz put it: "The myth, entirely unbelievable for anyone who was there, irrespective of side, that Austria was a victim and not an agent of fascism, undoubtedly brought political advantages, but caused a blunting of intelligence and other psychic damage among those who suddenly began to believe it themselves" (1992: 31, my trans.).

In the summer of 1976 Bronka and Joseph celebrated their fiftieth wedding anniversary at the home of Bronka's younger sister, in New Jersey. Joseph died that autumn. Bronka took an overdose of pills in a failed suicide attempt and spent the rest of her life in a New Jersey nursing home. She died in 1990, shortly before her ninety-first birthday.

References

Benz, Wolfgang, ed. 1994. *Das Exil der kleinen Leute: Alltagserfahrungen deutscher Juden in der Emigration.* Frankfurt a.M.: Fischer Taschenbuch Verlag.

Berghahn, Marion. 1984. "German Jews in England: Aspects of the Assimilation and Integration Process." In Hirschfeld, pp. 285–306.

———. 1988. *Continental Britains: German-Jewish Refugees from Nazi Germany.* New York: St. Martin's Press.

Botz, Gerhard. 1987. *The Jews of Vienna from the* Anschluss *to the Holocaust.* In Ivar Oxaal, Michael Pollak, and Gerhard Botz, eds., *Jews, Antisemitism, and Culture in Vienna*, pp. 185–204. London: Routledge and Kegan Paul.

———. 1990. "Probleme und Perspektiven: Einleitung der Herausgeber." In Botz, Oxaal, and Pollock, pp. 9–28.

Botz, Gerhard, Ivar Oxaal, and Michael Pollak, eds. 1990. *Eine zerstörte Kultur: Jüdisches Leben und Antisemitismus in Wien seit dem 19. Jahrhundert.* Buchloe: DVO.

Buruma, Ian. 1998. "The Afterlife of Anne Frank" Review article. *New York Review of Books*, February 19, pp. 4–8.

Clair, Jean. 1986. *Vienne, 1880–1938: L'apocalypse joyeuse.* Paris: Centre Pompidou.

Davidson, Jillian. 1991. "German-Jewish Women in England." In Mosse, pp. 533–51.

Düriegel, Günter. 1984. "Portrait of a City—Configuration and Change." In Waissenberger, pp. 9–30.

Ernst, Jimmy. 1984. *A Not-So-Still Life: A Memoir.* New York: St. Martin's/ Marek.

Freud, Anton Walter. 1993. "Antisemitismus war etwas natürliches, so daß man darüber nicht zu sprechen brauchte." In Wimmer, 1993, pp. 21–24.

Friedländer, Saul. 1997. *Nazi Germany and the Jews.* Vol. 1: *The Years of Persecution, 1933–1939.* New York: HarperCollins.

Furst, Desider. 1994. "The Isle of Man." In Furst and Furst, pp. 117–32.

Furst, Desider, and Lillian R. Furst. 1994. *Home Is Somewhere Else: Autobiography in Two Voices.* Albany: State University of New York Press.

Gaisbauer, Adolf, ed., with Doris Oppenheim-Liffman. 1996. *David Ernst Oppenheim: . . . 'von Eurem treuen Vater David.' David Ernst Oppenheim in seinen Briefen 1938–1942.* Vienna: Böhlau Verlag.

Gershon, Karen. 1966. *We Came as Children: A Collective Autobiography.* New York: Harcourt, Brace & World.

Gill, Lesley. 1994. *Precarious Dependencies: Gender, Class and Domestic Service in Bolivia.* New York: Columbia University Press.

Gillman, Peter, and Leni Gillman. 1980. *'Collar the Lot!' How Britain Interned and Expelled Its Wartime Refugees.* London: Quartet Books.

Heilbut, Anthony. 1983. *Exiled in Paradise: German Refugee Artists and Intellectuals in America from the 1930s to the Present.* New York: Viking.

Hirschfeld, Gerhard, ed. 1984. *Exile in Great Britain: Refugees from Hitler's Germany.* Warwick, UK: Berg Publishers, for the German Historical Institute, London.

Kochan, Miriam. 1983. *Britain's Internees in the Second World War.* London: Macmillan.

Kölmel, Rainer. 1984. "Problems of Settlement." In Hirschfeld, pp. 251–85.

Kranzler, David. 1976. *Japanese, Nazis and Jews: The Jewish Refugee Community of Shanghai, 1938–1945.* New York: Yeshiva University Press.

Kushner, Tony. 1988. "Asylum or Servitude? Refugee Domestics in Britain, 1933–1945." *Bulletin of the Society for the Study of Labour History* 53.

———. 1991. "An Alien Occupation—Jewish Refugees and Domestic Service in Britain, 1933–1948." In Julius Carlebach et al., eds., *Second Chance: Two Centuries of German-Speaking Jews in the United Kingdom,* pp. 553–78. Schriftenreihe wissenschaftlizner Abhandlungen des Leo Baeck Instituts, no. 48. Tübingen: J. C. B. Moher (Paul Siebeck).

Langness, L. L., and G. Frank. 1981. *Lives: An Anthropological Approach to Biography.* Novato, CA: Chandler and Sharp.

Mahler-Schächter, Edith. 1993. "In bezug auf Hitler haben wir Vogel Strauss gespielt." In Wimmer, pp. 59–64.

Mayer, Hans. 1982–84. *Ein Deutscher auf Widerruf: Erinnerungen.* 2 vols. Frankfurt a.M.: Suhrkamp.

———. 1994. *Widerruf: Über Deutsche und Juden.* Frankfurt a.M.: Suhrkamp.

Miller, Arthur. 1994. *Broken Glass: A Play.* New York: Penguin Books.

Mosse, X. 1991. [Info to come].

Myerhoff, Barbara. 1978. *Number Our Days.* New York: E. P. Dutton.

Myerhoff, Barbara, with Deena Metzger. 1992. *Remembered Lives: The Work of Ritual, Story Telling and Growing Old.* Ann Arbor: University of Michigan Press.

Nett, E.W. 1966. "The Servant Class in a Developing Country: Ecuador." *Journal of Inter-American Studies* 8: 437–52.

Oxaal, Ivaar. 1990. "Die Juden im Wien des jungen Hitler: Historische und soziologische Aspekte." In Botz, Oxaal, and Pollak, pp. 29–60.

Rollins, Judith. 1985. *Between Women: Domestics and Their Employers.* Philadelphia: Temple University Press.

Sanjek, Roger, and Shellee Cohen, eds. 1990. *At Work in Homes: Household Work in World Perspective.* American Ethnological Society Monograph Series, no. 3. Washington, D.C.: American Anthropological Association.

Sayle, Murray. 1997. "Spying Doesn't Get Any Better Than This." Review of *Stalin's Spy: Richard Sorge and the Tokyo Espionage Ring,* by Robert Whymant. *London Review of Books,* May 22, pp. 13–15.

Schorske, Carl E. 1980. *Fin-de-Siècle Vienna: Politics and Culture.* New York: Knopf.

Schwarz, Egon. 1992. *Keine Zeit für Eichendorff: Chronik unfreiwilliger Wanderjahre.* Frankfurt a.M.: Büchergilde Gutenberg.

Segal, Lore. 1964. *Other People's Houses: A Novel.* New York: Harcourt, Brace & World.

Seyfert, Michael. 1984. "His Majesty's Most Loyal Internees." In Hirschfeld, pp. 163–94.

Taylor, Pam. 1980. "Daughters and Mothers—Maids and Mistresses: Domestic Service between the Wars." In John Clarke, Chas Critcher, and Richard Johnson, eds., *Working Class Culture: Studies in History and Theory,* pp. 121–31. New York: St. Martin's Press.

Teveth, Shabtai. 1997. *Ben-Gurion and the Holocaust.* New York: Harcourt, Brace & Co.

Trahan, Elizabeth W. 1997a. *Geisterbeschwörung: Eine jüdische Jugend im Wien der Kriegsjahre.* Vienna: Picus.

———. 1997b. *Living with Ghosts.* New York: Peter Lang.

Waissenberger, Robert. 1984. *Vienna, 1890–1920.* New York: Rizzoli.

Walter, Hans Albert 1992. "Rollender Stein setzt kein Moos as: Das unge-
wöhnliche Leben des Literaturwissenschaftlers Egon Schwarz." In Schwarz,
pp. 345–76.

Whiteman, Dorit Bader. 1993. *The Uprooted: A Hitler Legacy: Voices of Those
Who Escaped before the "Final Solution."* New York: Insight Books.

Wimmer, Adi. 1990. " 'Expelled and Banished': The Exile Experience of Aus-
trian *Anschluss* Victims in Personal Histories and Literary Documents."
Journal of European Studies 20: 343–63.

———, ed. 1993. *Die Heimat wurde ihnen fremd, die Fremde nicht zur Heimat.*
Vienna: Verlag für Gesellschaftskritik.

Oil painting of Bronka, age eight, Cracow

Bronka, on a visit to her sister, Belgian sea coast, 1937

Bronka's parents, Lasarus and Anna Eichhorn, Vienna, ca. 1930

Joseph with the dog Sheila, "Yearkerscleugh," Scotland, 1939

Bronka and Joseph, Peoria, May 1948

Bronka with her four-year-old nephew Larry in South Orange, NJ, 1948

A Jewish man scrubbing a Vienna street in 1938. Part of Alfred Hrdlicka's "monument of admonishment against war and fascism," near the Vienna State Opera

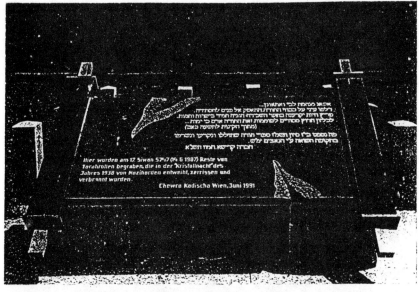

Burial of Torah scrolls destroyed during Kristallnacht, November 10, 1938.
Central Cemetery, Vienna, Jewish section